THIS BOOK BELONGS TO

_____

TRADING LOG

THIS BOOK WILL HELP TO KEEP YOUR TRADES ORGANISED, AND SHOW YOUR PROGRESS.

THIS BOOK INCLUDES 500 BLANK TRADING LOGS, SO YOU CAN RECORD EVERY DETAILS OF EVERY TRADE.

USE THE LOG TO RECORD:

- ORDER DATE.
- WHICH TYPE/SYMBOL - EG, BTC OR GBP/USD.
- ORDER NUMBER.
- BUY OR SELL.
- TRADE SIZE - EG, $1, $5, $20.
- ENTRY PRICE AND EXIT PRICE.
- TRADE CLOSE DATE.
- PROFIT OR LOSS.
- NEW BALANCE TOTAL.

USE THE GRID PAGES TO:

- PLOT SUPPORT AND RESISTANCE AREAS.
- SKETCH OUT HELPFUL CANDLESTICK PATTERNS.
- CHART YOUR OWN STRATEGIES.
- PLAN FUTURE TRADES AND ENTRY POINTS.

TRADING LOG

ORDER DATE/TIME	TYPE	ORDER #	BUY/SELL	SIZE	ENTRY PRICE	EXIT PRICE	CLOSE DATE /TIME	PROFIT/LOSS
20/01/20	BTC	2748394	BUY	$5	8602	8702	20/01/20	$500

NOTES: SUPPORT HELD PERFECTLY	NEW BALANCE
	$37000

ORDER DATE/TIME	TYPE	ORDER #	BUY/SELL	SIZE	ENTRY PRICE	EXIT PRICE	CLOSE DATE /TIME	PROFIT/LOSS

NOTES:	NEW BALANCE

ORDER DATE/TIME	TYPE	ORDER #	BUY/SELL	SIZE	ENTRY PRICE	EXIT PRICE	CLOSE DATE /TIME	PROFIT/LOSS

NOTES:	NEW BALANCE

ORDER DATE/TIME	TYPE	ORDER #	BUY/SELL	SIZE	ENTRY PRICE	EXIT PRICE	CLOSE DATE /TIME	PROFIT/LOSS

NOTES:	NEW BALANCE

ORDER DATE/TIME	TYPE	ORDER #	BUY/SELL	SIZE	ENTRY PRICE	EXIT PRICE	CLOSE DATE /TIME	PROFIT/LOSS

NOTES:	NEW BALANCE

TRADING LOG

ORDER DATE/TIME	TYPE	ORDER #	BUY/ SELL	SIZE	ENTRY PRICE	EXIT PRICE	CLOSE DATE /TIME	PROFIT/ LOSS

NOTES:	NEW BALANCE

ORDER DATE/TIME	TYPE	ORDER #	BUY/ SELL	SIZE	ENTRY PRICE	EXIT PRICE	CLOSE DATE /TIME	PROFIT/ LOSS

NOTES:	NEW BALANCE

ORDER DATE/TIME	TYPE	ORDER #	BUY/ SELL	SIZE	ENTRY PRICE	EXIT PRICE	CLOSE DATE /TIME	PROFIT/ LOSS

NOTES:	NEW BALANCE

ORDER DATE/TIME	TYPE	ORDER #	BUY/ SELL	SIZE	ENTRY PRICE	EXIT PRICE	CLOSE DATE /TIME	PROFIT/ LOSS

NOTES:	NEW BALANCE

ORDER DATE/TIME	TYPE	ORDER #	BUY/ SELL	SIZE	ENTRY PRICE	EXIT PRICE	CLOSE DATE /TIME	PROFIT/ LOSS

NOTES:	NEW BALANCE

TRADING LOG

ORDER DATE/TIME	TYPE	ORDER #	BUY/ SELL	SIZE	ENTRY PRICE	EXIT PRICE	CLOSE DATE /TIME	PROFIT/ LOSS

NOTES:	NEW BALANCE

ORDER DATE/TIME	TYPE	ORDER #	BUY/ SELL	SIZE	ENTRY PRICE	EXIT PRICE	CLOSE DATE /TIME	PROFIT/ LOSS

NOTES:	NEW BALANCE

ORDER DATE/TIME	TYPE	ORDER #	BUY/ SELL	SIZE	ENTRY PRICE	EXIT PRICE	CLOSE DATE /TIME	PROFIT/ LOSS

NOTES:	NEW BALANCE

ORDER DATE/TIME	TYPE	ORDER #	BUY/ SELL	SIZE	ENTRY PRICE	EXIT PRICE	CLOSE DATE /TIME	PROFIT/ LOSS

NOTES:	NEW BALANCE

ORDER DATE/TIME	TYPE	ORDER #	BUY/ SELL	SIZE	ENTRY PRICE	EXIT PRICE	CLOSE DATE /TIME	PROFIT/ LOSS

NOTES:	NEW BALANCE

TRADING LOG

ORDER DATE/TIME	TYPE	ORDER #	BUY/SELL	SIZE	ENTRY PRICE	EXIT PRICE	CLOSE DATE /TIME	PROFIT/LOSS

NOTES:				NEW BALANCE	

ORDER DATE/TIME	TYPE	ORDER #	BUY/SELL	SIZE	ENTRY PRICE	EXIT PRICE	CLOSE DATE /TIME	PROFIT/LOSS

NOTES:				NEW BALANCE	

ORDER DATE/TIME	TYPE	ORDER #	BUY/SELL	SIZE	ENTRY PRICE	EXIT PRICE	CLOSE DATE /TIME	PROFIT/LOSS

NOTES:				NEW BALANCE	

ORDER DATE/TIME	TYPE	ORDER #	BUY/SELL	SIZE	ENTRY PRICE	EXIT PRICE	CLOSE DATE /TIME	PROFIT/LOSS

NOTES:				NEW BALANCE	

ORDER DATE/TIME	TYPE	ORDER #	BUY/SELL	SIZE	ENTRY PRICE	EXIT PRICE	CLOSE DATE /TIME	PROFIT/LOSS

NOTES:				NEW BALANCE	

TRADING LOG

ORDER DATE/TIME	TYPE	ORDER #	BUY/ SELL	SIZE	ENTRY PRICE	EXIT PRICE	CLOSE DATE /TIME	PROFIT/ LOSS

NOTES:	NEW BALANCE

ORDER DATE/TIME	TYPE	ORDER #	BUY/ SELL	SIZE	ENTRY PRICE	EXIT PRICE	CLOSE DATE /TIME	PROFIT/ LOSS

NOTES:	NEW BALANCE

ORDER DATE/TIME	TYPE	ORDER #	BUY/ SELL	SIZE	ENTRY PRICE	EXIT PRICE	CLOSE DATE /TIME	PROFIT/ LOSS

NOTES:	NEW BALANCE

ORDER DATE/TIME	TYPE	ORDER #	BUY/ SELL	SIZE	ENTRY PRICE	EXIT PRICE	CLOSE DATE /TIME	PROFIT/ LOSS

NOTES:	NEW BALANCE

ORDER DATE/TIME	TYPE	ORDER #	BUY/ SELL	SIZE	ENTRY PRICE	EXIT PRICE	CLOSE DATE /TIME	PROFIT/ LOSS

NOTES:	NEW BALANCE

TRADING LOG

ORDER DATE/TIME	TYPE	ORDER #	BUY/ SELL	SIZE	ENTRY PRICE	EXIT PRICE	CLOSE DATE /TIME	PROFIT/ LOSS

NOTES:		NEW BALANCE

ORDER DATE/TIME	TYPE	ORDER #	BUY/ SELL	SIZE	ENTRY PRICE	EXIT PRICE	CLOSE DATE /TIME	PROFIT/ LOSS

NOTES:		NEW BALANCE

ORDER DATE/TIME	TYPE	ORDER #	BUY/ SELL	SIZE	ENTRY PRICE	EXIT PRICE	CLOSE DATE /TIME	PROFIT/ LOSS

NOTES:		NEW BALANCE

ORDER DATE/TIME	TYPE	ORDER #	BUY/ SELL	SIZE	ENTRY PRICE	EXIT PRICE	CLOSE DATE /TIME	PROFIT/ LOSS

NOTES:		NEW BALANCE

ORDER DATE/TIME	TYPE	ORDER #	BUY/ SELL	SIZE	ENTRY PRICE	EXIT PRICE	CLOSE DATE /TIME	PROFIT/ LOSS

NOTES:		NEW BALANCE

TRADING LOG

ORDER DATE/TIME	TYPE	ORDER #	BUY/ SELL	SIZE	ENTRY PRICE	EXIT PRICE	CLOSE DATE /TIME	PROFIT/ LOSS

NOTES:	NEW BALANCE

ORDER DATE/TIME	TYPE	ORDER #	BUY/ SELL	SIZE	ENTRY PRICE	EXIT PRICE	CLOSE DATE /TIME	PROFIT/ LOSS

NOTES:	NEW BALANCE

ORDER DATE/TIME	TYPE	ORDER #	BUY/ SELL	SIZE	ENTRY PRICE	EXIT PRICE	CLOSE DATE /TIME	PROFIT/ LOSS

NOTES:	NEW BALANCE

ORDER DATE/TIME	TYPE	ORDER #	BUY/ SELL	SIZE	ENTRY PRICE	EXIT PRICE	CLOSE DATE /TIME	PROFIT/ LOSS

NOTES:	NEW BALANCE

ORDER DATE/TIME	TYPE	ORDER #	BUY/ SELL	SIZE	ENTRY PRICE	EXIT PRICE	CLOSE DATE /TIME	PROFIT/ LOSS

NOTES:	NEW BALANCE

TRADING LOG

ORDER DATE/TIME	TYPE	ORDER #	BUY/ SELL	SIZE	ENTRY PRICE	EXIT PRICE	CLOSE DATE /TIME	PROFIT/ LOSS

NOTES:	NEW BALANCE

ORDER DATE/TIME	TYPE	ORDER #	BUY/ SELL	SIZE	ENTRY PRICE	EXIT PRICE	CLOSE DATE /TIME	PROFIT/ LOSS

NOTES:	NEW BALANCE

ORDER DATE/TIME	TYPE	ORDER #	BUY/ SELL	SIZE	ENTRY PRICE	EXIT PRICE	CLOSE DATE /TIME	PROFIT/ LOSS

NOTES:	NEW BALANCE

ORDER DATE/TIME	TYPE	ORDER #	BUY/ SELL	SIZE	ENTRY PRICE	EXIT PRICE	CLOSE DATE /TIME	PROFIT/ LOSS

NOTES:	NEW BALANCE

ORDER DATE/TIME	TYPE	ORDER #	BUY/ SELL	SIZE	ENTRY PRICE	EXIT PRICE	CLOSE DATE /TIME	PROFIT/ LOSS

NOTES:	NEW BALANCE

TRADING LOG

ORDER DATE/TIME	TYPE	ORDER #	BUY/ SELL	SIZE	ENTRY PRICE	EXIT PRICE	CLOSE DATE /TIME	PROFIT/ LOSS

NOTES:					NEW BALANCE			

ORDER DATE/TIME	TYPE	ORDER #	BUY/ SELL	SIZE	ENTRY PRICE	EXIT PRICE	CLOSE DATE /TIME	PROFIT/ LOSS

NOTES:					NEW BALANCE			

ORDER DATE/TIME	TYPE	ORDER #	BUY/ SELL	SIZE	ENTRY PRICE	EXIT PRICE	CLOSE DATE /TIME	PROFIT/ LOSS

NOTES:					NEW BALANCE			

ORDER DATE/TIME	TYPE	ORDER #	BUY/ SELL	SIZE	ENTRY PRICE	EXIT PRICE	CLOSE DATE /TIME	PROFIT/ LOSS

NOTES:					NEW BALANCE			

ORDER DATE/TIME	TYPE	ORDER #	BUY/ SELL	SIZE	ENTRY PRICE	EXIT PRICE	CLOSE DATE /TIME	PROFIT/ LOSS

NOTES:					NEW BALANCE			

TRADING LOG

ORDER DATE/TIME	TYPE	ORDER #	BUY/SELL	SIZE	ENTRY PRICE	EXIT PRICE	CLOSE DATE /TIME	PROFIT/LOSS

NOTES:	NEW BALANCE

ORDER DATE/TIME	TYPE	ORDER #	BUY/SELL	SIZE	ENTRY PRICE	EXIT PRICE	CLOSE DATE /TIME	PROFIT/LOSS

NOTES:	NEW BALANCE

ORDER DATE/TIME	TYPE	ORDER #	BUY/SELL	SIZE	ENTRY PRICE	EXIT PRICE	CLOSE DATE /TIME	PROFIT/LOSS

NOTES:	NEW BALANCE

ORDER DATE/TIME	TYPE	ORDER #	BUY/SELL	SIZE	ENTRY PRICE	EXIT PRICE	CLOSE DATE /TIME	PROFIT/LOSS

NOTES:	NEW BALANCE

ORDER DATE/TIME	TYPE	ORDER #	BUY/SELL	SIZE	ENTRY PRICE	EXIT PRICE	CLOSE DATE /TIME	PROFIT/LOSS

NOTES:	NEW BALANCE

TRADING LOG

ORDER DATE/TIME	TYPE	ORDER #	BUY/ SELL	SIZE	ENTRY PRICE	EXIT PRICE	CLOSE DATE /TIME	PROFIT/ LOSS

NOTES:		NEW BALANCE

ORDER DATE/TIME	TYPE	ORDER #	BUY/ SELL	SIZE	ENTRY PRICE	EXIT PRICE	CLOSE DATE /TIME	PROFIT/ LOSS

NOTES:		NEW BALANCE

ORDER DATE/TIME	TYPE	ORDER #	BUY/ SELL	SIZE	ENTRY PRICE	EXIT PRICE	CLOSE DATE /TIME	PROFIT/ LOSS

NOTES:		NEW BALANCE

ORDER DATE/TIME	TYPE	ORDER #	BUY/ SELL	SIZE	ENTRY PRICE	EXIT PRICE	CLOSE DATE /TIME	PROFIT/ LOSS

NOTES:		NEW BALANCE

ORDER DATE/TIME	TYPE	ORDER #	BUY/ SELL	SIZE	ENTRY PRICE	EXIT PRICE	CLOSE DATE /TIME	PROFIT/ LOSS

NOTES:		NEW BALANCE

TRADING LOG

ORDER DATE/TIME	TYPE	ORDER #	BUY/ SELL	SIZE	ENTRY PRICE	EXIT PRICE	CLOSE DATE /TIME	PROFIT/ LOSS

NOTES:		NEW BALANCE

ORDER DATE/TIME	TYPE	ORDER #	BUY/ SELL	SIZE	ENTRY PRICE	EXIT PRICE	CLOSE DATE /TIME	PROFIT/ LOSS

NOTES:		NEW BALANCE

ORDER DATE/TIME	TYPE	ORDER #	BUY/ SELL	SIZE	ENTRY PRICE	EXIT PRICE	CLOSE DATE /TIME	PROFIT/ LOSS

NOTES:		NEW BALANCE

ORDER DATE/TIME	TYPE	ORDER #	BUY/ SELL	SIZE	ENTRY PRICE	EXIT PRICE	CLOSE DATE /TIME	PROFIT/ LOSS

NOTES:		NEW BALANCE

ORDER DATE/TIME	TYPE	ORDER #	BUY/ SELL	SIZE	ENTRY PRICE	EXIT PRICE	CLOSE DATE /TIME	PROFIT/ LOSS

NOTES:		NEW BALANCE

TRADING LOG

ORDER DATE/TIME	TYPE	ORDER #	BUY/ SELL	SIZE	ENTRY PRICE	EXIT PRICE	CLOSE DATE /TIME	PROFIT/ LOSS

NOTES:	NEW BALANCE

ORDER DATE/TIME	TYPE	ORDER #	BUY/ SELL	SIZE	ENTRY PRICE	EXIT PRICE	CLOSE DATE /TIME	PROFIT/ LOSS

NOTES:	NEW BALANCE

ORDER DATE/TIME	TYPE	ORDER #	BUY/ SELL	SIZE	ENTRY PRICE	EXIT PRICE	CLOSE DATE /TIME	PROFIT/ LOSS

NOTES:	NEW BALANCE

ORDER DATE/TIME	TYPE	ORDER #	BUY/ SELL	SIZE	ENTRY PRICE	EXIT PRICE	CLOSE DATE /TIME	PROFIT/ LOSS

NOTES:	NEW BALANCE

ORDER DATE/TIME	TYPE	ORDER #	BUY/ SELL	SIZE	ENTRY PRICE	EXIT PRICE	CLOSE DATE /TIME	PROFIT/ LOSS

NOTES:	NEW BALANCE

TRADING LOG

ORDER DATE/TIME	TYPE	ORDER #	BUY/ SELL	SIZE	ENTRY PRICE	EXIT PRICE	CLOSE DATE /TIME	PROFIT/ LOSS

NOTES:	NEW BALANCE

ORDER DATE/TIME	TYPE	ORDER #	BUY/ SELL	SIZE	ENTRY PRICE	EXIT PRICE	CLOSE DATE /TIME	PROFIT/ LOSS

NOTES:	NEW BALANCE

ORDER DATE/TIME	TYPE	ORDER #	BUY/ SELL	SIZE	ENTRY PRICE	EXIT PRICE	CLOSE DATE /TIME	PROFIT/ LOSS

NOTES:	NEW BALANCE

ORDER DATE/TIME	TYPE	ORDER #	BUY/ SELL	SIZE	ENTRY PRICE	EXIT PRICE	CLOSE DATE /TIME	PROFIT/ LOSS

NOTES:	NEW BALANCE

ORDER DATE/TIME	TYPE	ORDER #	BUY/ SELL	SIZE	ENTRY PRICE	EXIT PRICE	CLOSE DATE /TIME	PROFIT/ LOSS

NOTES:	NEW BALANCE

TRADING LOG

ORDER DATE/TIME	TYPE	ORDER #	BUY/ SELL	SIZE	ENTRY PRICE	EXIT PRICE	CLOSE DATE /TIME	PROFIT/ LOSS

NOTES:	NEW BALANCE

ORDER DATE/TIME	TYPE	ORDER #	BUY/ SELL	SIZE	ENTRY PRICE	EXIT PRICE	CLOSE DATE /TIME	PROFIT/ LOSS

NOTES:	NEW BALANCE

ORDER DATE/TIME	TYPE	ORDER #	BUY/ SELL	SIZE	ENTRY PRICE	EXIT PRICE	CLOSE DATE /TIME	PROFIT/ LOSS

NOTES:	NEW BALANCE

ORDER DATE/TIME	TYPE	ORDER #	BUY/ SELL	SIZE	ENTRY PRICE	EXIT PRICE	CLOSE DATE /TIME	PROFIT/ LOSS

NOTES:	NEW BALANCE

ORDER DATE/TIME	TYPE	ORDER #	BUY/ SELL	SIZE	ENTRY PRICE	EXIT PRICE	CLOSE DATE /TIME	PROFIT/ LOSS

NOTES:	NEW BALANCE

TRADING LOG

ORDER DATE/TIME	TYPE	ORDER #	BUY/ SELL	SIZE	ENTRY PRICE	EXIT PRICE	CLOSE DATE /TIME	PROFIT/ LOSS

NOTES:		NEW BALANCE

ORDER DATE/TIME	TYPE	ORDER #	BUY/ SELL	SIZE	ENTRY PRICE	EXIT PRICE	CLOSE DATE /TIME	PROFIT/ LOSS

NOTES:		NEW BALANCE

ORDER DATE/TIME	TYPE	ORDER #	BUY/ SELL	SIZE	ENTRY PRICE	EXIT PRICE	CLOSE DATE /TIME	PROFIT/ LOSS

NOTES:		NEW BALANCE

ORDER DATE/TIME	TYPE	ORDER #	BUY/ SELL	SIZE	ENTRY PRICE	EXIT PRICE	CLOSE DATE /TIME	PROFIT/ LOSS

NOTES:		NEW BALANCE

ORDER DATE/TIME	TYPE	ORDER #	BUY/ SELL	SIZE	ENTRY PRICE	EXIT PRICE	CLOSE DATE /TIME	PROFIT/ LOSS

NOTES:		NEW BALANCE

TRADING LOG

ORDER DATE/TIME	TYPE	ORDER #	BUY/ SELL	SIZE	ENTRY PRICE	EXIT PRICE	CLOSE DATE /TIME	PROFIT/ LOSS

NOTES:						NEW BALANCE	

ORDER DATE/TIME	TYPE	ORDER #	BUY/ SELL	SIZE	ENTRY PRICE	EXIT PRICE	CLOSE DATE /TIME	PROFIT/ LOSS

NOTES:						NEW BALANCE	

ORDER DATE/TIME	TYPE	ORDER #	BUY/ SELL	SIZE	ENTRY PRICE	EXIT PRICE	CLOSE DATE /TIME	PROFIT/ LOSS

NOTES:						NEW BALANCE	

ORDER DATE/TIME	TYPE	ORDER #	BUY/ SELL	SIZE	ENTRY PRICE	EXIT PRICE	CLOSE DATE /TIME	PROFIT/ LOSS

NOTES:						NEW BALANCE	

ORDER DATE/TIME	TYPE	ORDER #	BUY/ SELL	SIZE	ENTRY PRICE	EXIT PRICE	CLOSE DATE /TIME	PROFIT/ LOSS

NOTES:						NEW BALANCE	

TRADING LOG

ORDER DATE/TIME	TYPE	ORDER #	BUY/ SELL	SIZE	ENTRY PRICE	EXIT PRICE	CLOSE DATE /TIME	PROFIT/ LOSS

NOTES:		NEW BALANCE

ORDER DATE/TIME	TYPE	ORDER #	BUY/ SELL	SIZE	ENTRY PRICE	EXIT PRICE	CLOSE DATE /TIME	PROFIT/ LOSS

NOTES:		NEW BALANCE

ORDER DATE/TIME	TYPE	ORDER #	BUY/ SELL	SIZE	ENTRY PRICE	EXIT PRICE	CLOSE DATE /TIME	PROFIT/ LOSS

NOTES:		NEW BALANCE

ORDER DATE/TIME	TYPE	ORDER #	BUY/ SELL	SIZE	ENTRY PRICE	EXIT PRICE	CLOSE DATE /TIME	PROFIT/ LOSS

NOTES:		NEW BALANCE

ORDER DATE/TIME	TYPE	ORDER #	BUY/ SELL	SIZE	ENTRY PRICE	EXIT PRICE	CLOSE DATE /TIME	PROFIT/ LOSS

NOTES:		NEW BALANCE

TRADING LOG

ORDER DATE/TIME	TYPE	ORDER #	BUY/ SELL	SIZE	ENTRY PRICE	EXIT PRICE	CLOSE DATE /TIME	PROFIT/ LOSS

NOTES:		NEW BALANCE

ORDER DATE/TIME	TYPE	ORDER #	BUY/ SELL	SIZE	ENTRY PRICE	EXIT PRICE	CLOSE DATE /TIME	PROFIT/ LOSS

NOTES:		NEW BALANCE

ORDER DATE/TIME	TYPE	ORDER #	BUY/ SELL	SIZE	ENTRY PRICE	EXIT PRICE	CLOSE DATE /TIME	PROFIT/ LOSS

NOTES:		NEW BALANCE

ORDER DATE/TIME	TYPE	ORDER #	BUY/ SELL	SIZE	ENTRY PRICE	EXIT PRICE	CLOSE DATE /TIME	PROFIT/ LOSS

NOTES:		NEW BALANCE

ORDER DATE/TIME	TYPE	ORDER #	BUY/ SELL	SIZE	ENTRY PRICE	EXIT PRICE	CLOSE DATE /TIME	PROFIT/ LOSS

NOTES:		NEW BALANCE

TRADING LOG

ORDER DATE/TIME	TYPE	ORDER #	BUY/ SELL	SIZE	ENTRY PRICE	EXIT PRICE	CLOSE DATE /TIME	PROFIT/ LOSS

NOTES:	NEW BALANCE

ORDER DATE/TIME	TYPE	ORDER #	BUY/ SELL	SIZE	ENTRY PRICE	EXIT PRICE	CLOSE DATE /TIME	PROFIT/ LOSS

NOTES:	NEW BALANCE

ORDER DATE/TIME	TYPE	ORDER #	BUY/ SELL	SIZE	ENTRY PRICE	EXIT PRICE	CLOSE DATE /TIME	PROFIT/ LOSS

NOTES:	NEW BALANCE

ORDER DATE/TIME	TYPE	ORDER #	BUY/ SELL	SIZE	ENTRY PRICE	EXIT PRICE	CLOSE DATE /TIME	PROFIT/ LOSS

NOTES:	NEW BALANCE

ORDER DATE/TIME	TYPE	ORDER #	BUY/ SELL	SIZE	ENTRY PRICE	EXIT PRICE	CLOSE DATE /TIME	PROFIT/ LOSS

NOTES:	NEW BALANCE

TRADING LOG

ORDER DATE/TIME	TYPE	ORDER #	BUY/ SELL	SIZE	ENTRY PRICE	EXIT PRICE	CLOSE DATE /TIME	PROFIT/ LOSS

NOTES:	NEW BALANCE

ORDER DATE/TIME	TYPE	ORDER #	BUY/ SELL	SIZE	ENTRY PRICE	EXIT PRICE	CLOSE DATE /TIME	PROFIT/ LOSS

NOTES:	NEW BALANCE

ORDER DATE/TIME	TYPE	ORDER #	BUY/ SELL	SIZE	ENTRY PRICE	EXIT PRICE	CLOSE DATE /TIME	PROFIT/ LOSS

NOTES:	NEW BALANCE

ORDER DATE/TIME	TYPE	ORDER #	BUY/ SELL	SIZE	ENTRY PRICE	EXIT PRICE	CLOSE DATE /TIME	PROFIT/ LOSS

NOTES:	NEW BALANCE

ORDER DATE/TIME	TYPE	ORDER #	BUY/ SELL	SIZE	ENTRY PRICE	EXIT PRICE	CLOSE DATE /TIME	PROFIT/ LOSS

NOTES:	NEW BALANCE

TRADING LOG

ORDER DATE/TIME	TYPE	ORDER #	BUY/ SELL	SIZE	ENTRY PRICE	EXIT PRICE	CLOSE DATE /TIME	PROFIT/ LOSS

NOTES:	NEW BALANCE

ORDER DATE/TIME	TYPE	ORDER #	BUY/ SELL	SIZE	ENTRY PRICE	EXIT PRICE	CLOSE DATE /TIME	PROFIT/ LOSS

NOTES:	NEW BALANCE

ORDER DATE/TIME	TYPE	ORDER #	BUY/ SELL	SIZE	ENTRY PRICE	EXIT PRICE	CLOSE DATE /TIME	PROFIT/ LOSS

NOTES:	NEW BALANCE

ORDER DATE/TIME	TYPE	ORDER #	BUY/ SELL	SIZE	ENTRY PRICE	EXIT PRICE	CLOSE DATE /TIME	PROFIT/ LOSS

NOTES:	NEW BALANCE

ORDER DATE/TIME	TYPE	ORDER #	BUY/ SELL	SIZE	ENTRY PRICE	EXIT PRICE	CLOSE DATE /TIME	PROFIT/ LOSS

NOTES:	NEW BALANCE

TRADING LOG

ORDER DATE/TIME	TYPE	ORDER #	BUY/ SELL	SIZE	ENTRY PRICE	EXIT PRICE	CLOSE DATE /TIME	PROFIT/ LOSS

NOTES:	NEW BALANCE

ORDER DATE/TIME	TYPE	ORDER #	BUY/ SELL	SIZE	ENTRY PRICE	EXIT PRICE	CLOSE DATE /TIME	PROFIT/ LOSS

NOTES:	NEW BALANCE

ORDER DATE/TIME	TYPE	ORDER #	BUY/ SELL	SIZE	ENTRY PRICE	EXIT PRICE	CLOSE DATE /TIME	PROFIT/ LOSS

NOTES:	NEW BALANCE

ORDER DATE/TIME	TYPE	ORDER #	BUY/ SELL	SIZE	ENTRY PRICE	EXIT PRICE	CLOSE DATE /TIME	PROFIT/ LOSS

NOTES:	NEW BALANCE

ORDER DATE/TIME	TYPE	ORDER #	BUY/ SELL	SIZE	ENTRY PRICE	EXIT PRICE	CLOSE DATE /TIME	PROFIT/ LOSS

NOTES:	NEW BALANCE

TRADING LOG

ORDER DATE/TIME	TYPE	ORDER #	BUY/ SELL	SIZE	ENTRY PRICE	EXIT PRICE	CLOSE DATE /TIME	PROFIT/ LOSS

NOTES:			NEW BALANCE

ORDER DATE/TIME	TYPE	ORDER #	BUY/ SELL	SIZE	ENTRY PRICE	EXIT PRICE	CLOSE DATE /TIME	PROFIT/ LOSS

NOTES:			NEW BALANCE

ORDER DATE/TIME	TYPE	ORDER #	BUY/ SELL	SIZE	ENTRY PRICE	EXIT PRICE	CLOSE DATE /TIME	PROFIT/ LOSS

NOTES:			NEW BALANCE

ORDER DATE/TIME	TYPE	ORDER #	BUY/ SELL	SIZE	ENTRY PRICE	EXIT PRICE	CLOSE DATE /TIME	PROFIT/ LOSS

NOTES:			NEW BALANCE

ORDER DATE/TIME	TYPE	ORDER #	BUY/ SELL	SIZE	ENTRY PRICE	EXIT PRICE	CLOSE DATE /TIME	PROFIT/ LOSS

NOTES:			NEW BALANCE

TRADING LOG

ORDER DATE/TIME	TYPE	ORDER #	BUY/ SELL	SIZE	ENTRY PRICE	EXIT PRICE	CLOSE DATE /TIME	PROFIT/ LOSS

NOTES:	NEW BALANCE

ORDER DATE/TIME	TYPE	ORDER #	BUY/ SELL	SIZE	ENTRY PRICE	EXIT PRICE	CLOSE DATE /TIME	PROFIT/ LOSS

NOTES:	NEW BALANCE

ORDER DATE/TIME	TYPE	ORDER #	BUY/ SELL	SIZE	ENTRY PRICE	EXIT PRICE	CLOSE DATE /TIME	PROFIT/ LOSS

NOTES:	NEW BALANCE

ORDER DATE/TIME	TYPE	ORDER #	BUY/ SELL	SIZE	ENTRY PRICE	EXIT PRICE	CLOSE DATE /TIME	PROFIT/ LOSS

NOTES:	NEW BALANCE

ORDER DATE/TIME	TYPE	ORDER #	BUY/ SELL	SIZE	ENTRY PRICE	EXIT PRICE	CLOSE DATE /TIME	PROFIT/ LOSS

NOTES:	NEW BALANCE

TRADING LOG

ORDER DATE/TIME	TYPE	ORDER #	BUY/ SELL	SIZE	ENTRY PRICE	EXIT PRICE	CLOSE DATE /TIME	PROFIT/ LOSS

NOTES:		NEW BALANCE

ORDER DATE/TIME	TYPE	ORDER #	BUY/ SELL	SIZE	ENTRY PRICE	EXIT PRICE	CLOSE DATE /TIME	PROFIT/ LOSS

NOTES:		NEW BALANCE

ORDER DATE/TIME	TYPE	ORDER #	BUY/ SELL	SIZE	ENTRY PRICE	EXIT PRICE	CLOSE DATE /TIME	PROFIT/ LOSS

NOTES:		NEW BALANCE

ORDER DATE/TIME	TYPE	ORDER #	BUY/ SELL	SIZE	ENTRY PRICE	EXIT PRICE	CLOSE DATE /TIME	PROFIT/ LOSS

NOTES:		NEW BALANCE

ORDER DATE/TIME	TYPE	ORDER #	BUY/ SELL	SIZE	ENTRY PRICE	EXIT PRICE	CLOSE DATE /TIME	PROFIT/ LOSS

NOTES:		NEW BALANCE

TRADING LOG

ORDER DATE/TIME	TYPE	ORDER #	BUY/ SELL	SIZE	ENTRY PRICE	EXIT PRICE	CLOSE DATE /TIME	PROFIT/ LOSS

NOTES:	NEW BALANCE

ORDER DATE/TIME	TYPE	ORDER #	BUY/ SELL	SIZE	ENTRY PRICE	EXIT PRICE	CLOSE DATE /TIME	PROFIT/ LOSS

NOTES:	NEW BALANCE

ORDER DATE/TIME	TYPE	ORDER #	BUY/ SELL	SIZE	ENTRY PRICE	EXIT PRICE	CLOSE DATE /TIME	PROFIT/ LOSS

NOTES:	NEW BALANCE

ORDER DATE/TIME	TYPE	ORDER #	BUY/ SELL	SIZE	ENTRY PRICE	EXIT PRICE	CLOSE DATE /TIME	PROFIT/ LOSS

NOTES:	NEW BALANCE

ORDER DATE/TIME	TYPE	ORDER #	BUY/ SELL	SIZE	ENTRY PRICE	EXIT PRICE	CLOSE DATE /TIME	PROFIT/ LOSS

NOTES:	NEW BALANCE

TRADING LOG

ORDER DATE/TIME	TYPE	ORDER #	BUY/ SELL	SIZE	ENTRY PRICE	EXIT PRICE	CLOSE DATE /TIME	PROFIT/ LOSS

NOTES:		NEW BALANCE

ORDER DATE/TIME	TYPE	ORDER #	BUY/ SELL	SIZE	ENTRY PRICE	EXIT PRICE	CLOSE DATE /TIME	PROFIT/ LOSS

NOTES:		NEW BALANCE

ORDER DATE/TIME	TYPE	ORDER #	BUY/ SELL	SIZE	ENTRY PRICE	EXIT PRICE	CLOSE DATE /TIME	PROFIT/ LOSS

NOTES:		NEW BALANCE

ORDER DATE/TIME	TYPE	ORDER #	BUY/ SELL	SIZE	ENTRY PRICE	EXIT PRICE	CLOSE DATE /TIME	PROFIT/ LOSS

NOTES:		NEW BALANCE

ORDER DATE/TIME	TYPE	ORDER #	BUY/ SELL	SIZE	ENTRY PRICE	EXIT PRICE	CLOSE DATE /TIME	PROFIT/ LOSS

NOTES:		NEW BALANCE

TRADING LOG

ORDER DATE/TIME	TYPE	ORDER #	BUY/ SELL	SIZE	ENTRY PRICE	EXIT PRICE	CLOSE DATE /TIME	PROFIT/ LOSS

NOTES:	NEW BALANCE

ORDER DATE/TIME	TYPE	ORDER #	BUY/ SELL	SIZE	ENTRY PRICE	EXIT PRICE	CLOSE DATE /TIME	PROFIT/ LOSS

NOTES:	NEW BALANCE

ORDER DATE/TIME	TYPE	ORDER #	BUY/ SELL	SIZE	ENTRY PRICE	EXIT PRICE	CLOSE DATE /TIME	PROFIT/ LOSS

NOTES:	NEW BALANCE

ORDER DATE/TIME	TYPE	ORDER #	BUY/ SELL	SIZE	ENTRY PRICE	EXIT PRICE	CLOSE DATE /TIME	PROFIT/ LOSS

NOTES:	NEW BALANCE

ORDER DATE/TIME	TYPE	ORDER #	BUY/ SELL	SIZE	ENTRY PRICE	EXIT PRICE	CLOSE DATE /TIME	PROFIT/ LOSS

NOTES:	NEW BALANCE

TRADING LOG

ORDER DATE/TIME	TYPE	ORDER #	BUY/ SELL	SIZE	ENTRY PRICE	EXIT PRICE	CLOSE DATE /TIME	PROFIT/ LOSS

NOTES:	NEW BALANCE

ORDER DATE/TIME	TYPE	ORDER #	BUY/ SELL	SIZE	ENTRY PRICE	EXIT PRICE	CLOSE DATE /TIME	PROFIT/ LOSS

NOTES:	NEW BALANCE

ORDER DATE/TIME	TYPE	ORDER #	BUY/ SELL	SIZE	ENTRY PRICE	EXIT PRICE	CLOSE DATE /TIME	PROFIT/ LOSS

NOTES:	NEW BALANCE

ORDER DATE/TIME	TYPE	ORDER #	BUY/ SELL	SIZE	ENTRY PRICE	EXIT PRICE	CLOSE DATE /TIME	PROFIT/ LOSS

NOTES:	NEW BALANCE

ORDER DATE/TIME	TYPE	ORDER #	BUY/ SELL	SIZE	ENTRY PRICE	EXIT PRICE	CLOSE DATE /TIME	PROFIT/ LOSS

NOTES:	NEW BALANCE

TRADING LOG

ORDER DATE/TIME	TYPE	ORDER #	BUY/ SELL	SIZE	ENTRY PRICE	EXIT PRICE	CLOSE DATE /TIME	PROFIT/ LOSS

NOTES:					NEW BALANCE	

ORDER DATE/TIME	TYPE	ORDER #	BUY/ SELL	SIZE	ENTRY PRICE	EXIT PRICE	CLOSE DATE /TIME	PROFIT/ LOSS

NOTES:					NEW BALANCE	

ORDER DATE/TIME	TYPE	ORDER #	BUY/ SELL	SIZE	ENTRY PRICE	EXIT PRICE	CLOSE DATE /TIME	PROFIT/ LOSS

NOTES:					NEW BALANCE	

ORDER DATE/TIME	TYPE	ORDER #	BUY/ SELL	SIZE	ENTRY PRICE	EXIT PRICE	CLOSE DATE /TIME	PROFIT/ LOSS

NOTES:					NEW BALANCE	

ORDER DATE/TIME	TYPE	ORDER #	BUY/ SELL	SIZE	ENTRY PRICE	EXIT PRICE	CLOSE DATE /TIME	PROFIT/ LOSS

NOTES:					NEW BALANCE	

TRADING LOG

ORDER DATE/TIME	TYPE	ORDER #	BUY/ SELL	SIZE	ENTRY PRICE	EXIT PRICE	CLOSE DATE /TIME	PROFIT/ LOSS

NOTES:	NEW BALANCE

ORDER DATE/TIME	TYPE	ORDER #	BUY/ SELL	SIZE	ENTRY PRICE	EXIT PRICE	CLOSE DATE /TIME	PROFIT/ LOSS

NOTES:	NEW BALANCE

ORDER DATE/TIME	TYPE	ORDER #	BUY/ SELL	SIZE	ENTRY PRICE	EXIT PRICE	CLOSE DATE /TIME	PROFIT/ LOSS

NOTES:	NEW BALANCE

ORDER DATE/TIME	TYPE	ORDER #	BUY/ SELL	SIZE	ENTRY PRICE	EXIT PRICE	CLOSE DATE /TIME	PROFIT/ LOSS

NOTES:	NEW BALANCE

ORDER DATE/TIME	TYPE	ORDER #	BUY/ SELL	SIZE	ENTRY PRICE	EXIT PRICE	CLOSE DATE /TIME	PROFIT/ LOSS

NOTES:	NEW BALANCE

TRADING LOG

ORDER DATE/TIME	TYPE	ORDER #	BUY/ SELL	SIZE	ENTRY PRICE	EXIT PRICE	CLOSE DATE /TIME	PROFIT/ LOSS

NOTES:	NEW BALANCE

ORDER DATE/TIME	TYPE	ORDER #	BUY/ SELL	SIZE	ENTRY PRICE	EXIT PRICE	CLOSE DATE /TIME	PROFIT/ LOSS

NOTES:	NEW BALANCE

ORDER DATE/TIME	TYPE	ORDER #	BUY/ SELL	SIZE	ENTRY PRICE	EXIT PRICE	CLOSE DATE /TIME	PROFIT/ LOSS

NOTES:	NEW BALANCE

ORDER DATE/TIME	TYPE	ORDER #	BUY/ SELL	SIZE	ENTRY PRICE	EXIT PRICE	CLOSE DATE /TIME	PROFIT/ LOSS

NOTES:	NEW BALANCE

ORDER DATE/TIME	TYPE	ORDER #	BUY/ SELL	SIZE	ENTRY PRICE	EXIT PRICE	CLOSE DATE /TIME	PROFIT/ LOSS

NOTES:	NEW BALANCE

TRADING LOG

ORDER DATE/TIME	TYPE	ORDER #	BUY/ SELL	SIZE	ENTRY PRICE	EXIT PRICE	CLOSE DATE /TIME	PROFIT/ LOSS

NOTES:	NEW BALANCE

ORDER DATE/TIME	TYPE	ORDER #	BUY/ SELL	SIZE	ENTRY PRICE	EXIT PRICE	CLOSE DATE /TIME	PROFIT/ LOSS

NOTES:	NEW BALANCE

ORDER DATE/TIME	TYPE	ORDER #	BUY/ SELL	SIZE	ENTRY PRICE	EXIT PRICE	CLOSE DATE /TIME	PROFIT/ LOSS

NOTES:	NEW BALANCE

ORDER DATE/TIME	TYPE	ORDER #	BUY/ SELL	SIZE	ENTRY PRICE	EXIT PRICE	CLOSE DATE /TIME	PROFIT/ LOSS

NOTES:	NEW BALANCE

ORDER DATE/TIME	TYPE	ORDER #	BUY/ SELL	SIZE	ENTRY PRICE	EXIT PRICE	CLOSE DATE /TIME	PROFIT/ LOSS

NOTES:	NEW BALANCE

TRADING LOG

ORDER DATE/TIME	TYPE	ORDER #	BUY/ SELL	SIZE	ENTRY PRICE	EXIT PRICE	CLOSE DATE /TIME	PROFIT/ LOSS

NOTES:	NEW BALANCE

ORDER DATE/TIME	TYPE	ORDER #	BUY/ SELL	SIZE	ENTRY PRICE	EXIT PRICE	CLOSE DATE /TIME	PROFIT/ LOSS

NOTES:	NEW BALANCE

ORDER DATE/TIME	TYPE	ORDER #	BUY/ SELL	SIZE	ENTRY PRICE	EXIT PRICE	CLOSE DATE /TIME	PROFIT/ LOSS

NOTES:	NEW BALANCE

ORDER DATE/TIME	TYPE	ORDER #	BUY/ SELL	SIZE	ENTRY PRICE	EXIT PRICE	CLOSE DATE /TIME	PROFIT/ LOSS

NOTES:	NEW BALANCE

ORDER DATE/TIME	TYPE	ORDER #	BUY/ SELL	SIZE	ENTRY PRICE	EXIT PRICE	CLOSE DATE /TIME	PROFIT/ LOSS

NOTES:	NEW BALANCE

TRADING LOG

ORDER DATE/TIME	TYPE	ORDER #	BUY/ SELL	SIZE	ENTRY PRICE	EXIT PRICE	CLOSE DATE /TIME	PROFIT/ LOSS

NOTES:					NEW BALANCE	

ORDER DATE/TIME	TYPE	ORDER #	BUY/ SELL	SIZE	ENTRY PRICE	EXIT PRICE	CLOSE DATE /TIME	PROFIT/ LOSS

NOTES:					NEW BALANCE	

ORDER DATE/TIME	TYPE	ORDER #	BUY/ SELL	SIZE	ENTRY PRICE	EXIT PRICE	CLOSE DATE /TIME	PROFIT/ LOSS

NOTES:					NEW BALANCE	

ORDER DATE/TIME	TYPE	ORDER #	BUY/ SELL	SIZE	ENTRY PRICE	EXIT PRICE	CLOSE DATE /TIME	PROFIT/ LOSS

NOTES:					NEW BALANCE	

ORDER DATE/TIME	TYPE	ORDER #	BUY/ SELL	SIZE	ENTRY PRICE	EXIT PRICE	CLOSE DATE /TIME	PROFIT/ LOSS

NOTES:					NEW BALANCE	

TRADING LOG

ORDER DATE/TIME	TYPE	ORDER #	BUY/ SELL	SIZE	ENTRY PRICE	EXIT PRICE	CLOSE DATE /TIME	PROFIT/ LOSS

NOTES:	NEW BALANCE

ORDER DATE/TIME	TYPE	ORDER #	BUY/ SELL	SIZE	ENTRY PRICE	EXIT PRICE	CLOSE DATE /TIME	PROFIT/ LOSS

NOTES:	NEW BALANCE

ORDER DATE/TIME	TYPE	ORDER #	BUY/ SELL	SIZE	ENTRY PRICE	EXIT PRICE	CLOSE DATE /TIME	PROFIT/ LOSS

NOTES:	NEW BALANCE

ORDER DATE/TIME	TYPE	ORDER #	BUY/ SELL	SIZE	ENTRY PRICE	EXIT PRICE	CLOSE DATE /TIME	PROFIT/ LOSS

NOTES:	NEW BALANCE

ORDER DATE/TIME	TYPE	ORDER #	BUY/ SELL	SIZE	ENTRY PRICE	EXIT PRICE	CLOSE DATE /TIME	PROFIT/ LOSS

NOTES:	NEW BALANCE

TRADING LOG

ORDER DATE/TIME	TYPE	ORDER #	BUY/ SELL	SIZE	ENTRY PRICE	EXIT PRICE	CLOSE DATE /TIME	PROFIT/ LOSS

NOTES:	NEW BALANCE

ORDER DATE/TIME	TYPE	ORDER #	BUY/ SELL	SIZE	ENTRY PRICE	EXIT PRICE	CLOSE DATE /TIME	PROFIT/ LOSS

NOTES:	NEW BALANCE

ORDER DATE/TIME	TYPE	ORDER #	BUY/ SELL	SIZE	ENTRY PRICE	EXIT PRICE	CLOSE DATE /TIME	PROFIT/ LOSS

NOTES:	NEW BALANCE

ORDER DATE/TIME	TYPE	ORDER #	BUY/ SELL	SIZE	ENTRY PRICE	EXIT PRICE	CLOSE DATE /TIME	PROFIT/ LOSS

NOTES:	NEW BALANCE

ORDER DATE/TIME	TYPE	ORDER #	BUY/ SELL	SIZE	ENTRY PRICE	EXIT PRICE	CLOSE DATE /TIME	PROFIT/ LOSS

NOTES:	NEW BALANCE

TRADING LOG

ORDER DATE/TIME	TYPE	ORDER #	BUY/ SELL	SIZE	ENTRY PRICE	EXIT PRICE	CLOSE DATE /TIME	PROFIT/ LOSS

NOTES:	NEW BALANCE

ORDER DATE/TIME	TYPE	ORDER #	BUY/ SELL	SIZE	ENTRY PRICE	EXIT PRICE	CLOSE DATE /TIME	PROFIT/ LOSS

NOTES:	NEW BALANCE

ORDER DATE/TIME	TYPE	ORDER #	BUY/ SELL	SIZE	ENTRY PRICE	EXIT PRICE	CLOSE DATE /TIME	PROFIT/ LOSS

NOTES:	NEW BALANCE

ORDER DATE/TIME	TYPE	ORDER #	BUY/ SELL	SIZE	ENTRY PRICE	EXIT PRICE	CLOSE DATE /TIME	PROFIT/ LOSS

NOTES:	NEW BALANCE

ORDER DATE/TIME	TYPE	ORDER #	BUY/ SELL	SIZE	ENTRY PRICE	EXIT PRICE	CLOSE DATE /TIME	PROFIT/ LOSS

NOTES:	NEW BALANCE

TRADING LOG

ORDER DATE/TIME	TYPE	ORDER #	BUY/ SELL	SIZE	ENTRY PRICE	EXIT PRICE	CLOSE DATE /TIME	PROFIT/ LOSS

NOTES:	NEW BALANCE

ORDER DATE/TIME	TYPE	ORDER #	BUY/ SELL	SIZE	ENTRY PRICE	EXIT PRICE	CLOSE DATE /TIME	PROFIT/ LOSS

NOTES:	NEW BALANCE

ORDER DATE/TIME	TYPE	ORDER #	BUY/ SELL	SIZE	ENTRY PRICE	EXIT PRICE	CLOSE DATE /TIME	PROFIT/ LOSS

NOTES:	NEW BALANCE

ORDER DATE/TIME	TYPE	ORDER #	BUY/ SELL	SIZE	ENTRY PRICE	EXIT PRICE	CLOSE DATE /TIME	PROFIT/ LOSS

NOTES:	NEW BALANCE

ORDER DATE/TIME	TYPE	ORDER #	BUY/ SELL	SIZE	ENTRY PRICE	EXIT PRICE	CLOSE DATE /TIME	PROFIT/ LOSS

NOTES:	NEW BALANCE

TRADING LOG

ORDER DATE/TIME	TYPE	ORDER #	BUY/ SELL	SIZE	ENTRY PRICE	EXIT PRICE	CLOSE DATE /TIME	PROFIT/ LOSS

NOTES:	NEW BALANCE

ORDER DATE/TIME	TYPE	ORDER #	BUY/ SELL	SIZE	ENTRY PRICE	EXIT PRICE	CLOSE DATE /TIME	PROFIT/ LOSS

NOTES:	NEW BALANCE

ORDER DATE/TIME	TYPE	ORDER #	BUY/ SELL	SIZE	ENTRY PRICE	EXIT PRICE	CLOSE DATE /TIME	PROFIT/ LOSS

NOTES:	NEW BALANCE

ORDER DATE/TIME	TYPE	ORDER #	BUY/ SELL	SIZE	ENTRY PRICE	EXIT PRICE	CLOSE DATE /TIME	PROFIT/ LOSS

NOTES:	NEW BALANCE

ORDER DATE/TIME	TYPE	ORDER #	BUY/ SELL	SIZE	ENTRY PRICE	EXIT PRICE	CLOSE DATE /TIME	PROFIT/ LOSS

NOTES:	NEW BALANCE

TRADING LOG

ORDER DATE/TIME	TYPE	ORDER #	BUY/ SELL	SIZE	ENTRY PRICE	EXIT PRICE	CLOSE DATE /TIME	PROFIT/ LOSS

NOTES:		NEW BALANCE

ORDER DATE/TIME	TYPE	ORDER #	BUY/ SELL	SIZE	ENTRY PRICE	EXIT PRICE	CLOSE DATE /TIME	PROFIT/ LOSS

NOTES:		NEW BALANCE

ORDER DATE/TIME	TYPE	ORDER #	BUY/ SELL	SIZE	ENTRY PRICE	EXIT PRICE	CLOSE DATE /TIME	PROFIT/ LOSS

NOTES:		NEW BALANCE

ORDER DATE/TIME	TYPE	ORDER #	BUY/ SELL	SIZE	ENTRY PRICE	EXIT PRICE	CLOSE DATE /TIME	PROFIT/ LOSS

NOTES:		NEW BALANCE

ORDER DATE/TIME	TYPE	ORDER #	BUY/ SELL	SIZE	ENTRY PRICE	EXIT PRICE	CLOSE DATE /TIME	PROFIT/ LOSS

NOTES:		NEW BALANCE

TRADING LOG

ORDER DATE/TIME	TYPE	ORDER #	BUY/ SELL	SIZE	ENTRY PRICE	EXIT PRICE	CLOSE DATE /TIME	PROFIT/ LOSS

NOTES:	NEW BALANCE

ORDER DATE/TIME	TYPE	ORDER #	BUY/ SELL	SIZE	ENTRY PRICE	EXIT PRICE	CLOSE DATE /TIME	PROFIT/ LOSS

NOTES:	NEW BALANCE

ORDER DATE/TIME	TYPE	ORDER #	BUY/ SELL	SIZE	ENTRY PRICE	EXIT PRICE	CLOSE DATE /TIME	PROFIT/ LOSS

NOTES:	NEW BALANCE

ORDER DATE/TIME	TYPE	ORDER #	BUY/ SELL	SIZE	ENTRY PRICE	EXIT PRICE	CLOSE DATE /TIME	PROFIT/ LOSS

NOTES:	NEW BALANCE

ORDER DATE/TIME	TYPE	ORDER #	BUY/ SELL	SIZE	ENTRY PRICE	EXIT PRICE	CLOSE DATE /TIME	PROFIT/ LOSS

NOTES:	NEW BALANCE

TRADING LOG

ORDER DATE/TIME	TYPE	ORDER #	BUY/ SELL	SIZE	ENTRY PRICE	EXIT PRICE	CLOSE DATE /TIME	PROFIT/ LOSS

NOTES:			NEW BALANCE	

ORDER DATE/TIME	TYPE	ORDER #	BUY/ SELL	SIZE	ENTRY PRICE	EXIT PRICE	CLOSE DATE /TIME	PROFIT/ LOSS

NOTES:			NEW BALANCE	

ORDER DATE/TIME	TYPE	ORDER #	BUY/ SELL	SIZE	ENTRY PRICE	EXIT PRICE	CLOSE DATE /TIME	PROFIT/ LOSS

NOTES:			NEW BALANCE	

ORDER DATE/TIME	TYPE	ORDER #	BUY/ SELL	SIZE	ENTRY PRICE	EXIT PRICE	CLOSE DATE /TIME	PROFIT/ LOSS

NOTES:			NEW BALANCE	

ORDER DATE/TIME	TYPE	ORDER #	BUY/ SELL	SIZE	ENTRY PRICE	EXIT PRICE	CLOSE DATE /TIME	PROFIT/ LOSS

NOTES:			NEW BALANCE	

TRADING LOG

ORDER DATE/TIME	TYPE	ORDER #	BUY/ SELL	SIZE	ENTRY PRICE	EXIT PRICE	CLOSE DATE /TIME	PROFIT/ LOSS

NOTES:	NEW BALANCE

ORDER DATE/TIME	TYPE	ORDER #	BUY/ SELL	SIZE	ENTRY PRICE	EXIT PRICE	CLOSE DATE /TIME	PROFIT/ LOSS

NOTES:	NEW BALANCE

ORDER DATE/TIME	TYPE	ORDER #	BUY/ SELL	SIZE	ENTRY PRICE	EXIT PRICE	CLOSE DATE /TIME	PROFIT/ LOSS

NOTES:	NEW BALANCE

ORDER DATE/TIME	TYPE	ORDER #	BUY/ SELL	SIZE	ENTRY PRICE	EXIT PRICE	CLOSE DATE /TIME	PROFIT/ LOSS

NOTES:	NEW BALANCE

ORDER DATE/TIME	TYPE	ORDER #	BUY/ SELL	SIZE	ENTRY PRICE	EXIT PRICE	CLOSE DATE /TIME	PROFIT/ LOSS

NOTES:	NEW BALANCE

TRADING LOG

ORDER DATE/TIME	TYPE	ORDER #	BUY/ SELL	SIZE	ENTRY PRICE	EXIT PRICE	CLOSE DATE /TIME	PROFIT/ LOSS

NOTES:					NEW BALANCE	

ORDER DATE/TIME	TYPE	ORDER #	BUY/ SELL	SIZE	ENTRY PRICE	EXIT PRICE	CLOSE DATE /TIME	PROFIT/ LOSS

NOTES:					NEW BALANCE	

ORDER DATE/TIME	TYPE	ORDER #	BUY/ SELL	SIZE	ENTRY PRICE	EXIT PRICE	CLOSE DATE /TIME	PROFIT/ LOSS

NOTES:					NEW BALANCE	

ORDER DATE/TIME	TYPE	ORDER #	BUY/ SELL	SIZE	ENTRY PRICE	EXIT PRICE	CLOSE DATE /TIME	PROFIT/ LOSS

NOTES:					NEW BALANCE	

ORDER DATE/TIME	TYPE	ORDER #	BUY/ SELL	SIZE	ENTRY PRICE	EXIT PRICE	CLOSE DATE /TIME	PROFIT/ LOSS

NOTES:					NEW BALANCE	

TRADING LOG

ORDER DATE/TIME	TYPE	ORDER #	BUY/ SELL	SIZE	ENTRY PRICE	EXIT PRICE	CLOSE DATE /TIME	PROFIT/ LOSS

NOTES:				NEW BALANCE	

ORDER DATE/TIME	TYPE	ORDER #	BUY/ SELL	SIZE	ENTRY PRICE	EXIT PRICE	CLOSE DATE /TIME	PROFIT/ LOSS

NOTES:				NEW BALANCE	

ORDER DATE/TIME	TYPE	ORDER #	BUY/ SELL	SIZE	ENTRY PRICE	EXIT PRICE	CLOSE DATE /TIME	PROFIT/ LOSS

NOTES:				NEW BALANCE	

ORDER DATE/TIME	TYPE	ORDER #	BUY/ SELL	SIZE	ENTRY PRICE	EXIT PRICE	CLOSE DATE /TIME	PROFIT/ LOSS

NOTES:				NEW BALANCE	

ORDER DATE/TIME	TYPE	ORDER #	BUY/ SELL	SIZE	ENTRY PRICE	EXIT PRICE	CLOSE DATE /TIME	PROFIT/ LOSS

NOTES:				NEW BALANCE	

TRADING LOG

ORDER DATE/TIME	TYPE	ORDER #	BUY/ SELL	SIZE	ENTRY PRICE	EXIT PRICE	CLOSE DATE /TIME	PROFIT/ LOSS

NOTES:				NEW BALANCE

ORDER DATE/TIME	TYPE	ORDER #	BUY/ SELL	SIZE	ENTRY PRICE	EXIT PRICE	CLOSE DATE /TIME	PROFIT/ LOSS

NOTES:				NEW BALANCE

ORDER DATE/TIME	TYPE	ORDER #	BUY/ SELL	SIZE	ENTRY PRICE	EXIT PRICE	CLOSE DATE /TIME	PROFIT/ LOSS

NOTES:				NEW BALANCE

ORDER DATE/TIME	TYPE	ORDER #	BUY/ SELL	SIZE	ENTRY PRICE	EXIT PRICE	CLOSE DATE /TIME	PROFIT/ LOSS

NOTES:				NEW BALANCE

ORDER DATE/TIME	TYPE	ORDER #	BUY/ SELL	SIZE	ENTRY PRICE	EXIT PRICE	CLOSE DATE /TIME	PROFIT/ LOSS

NOTES:				NEW BALANCE

TRADING LOG

ORDER DATE/TIME	TYPE	ORDER #	BUY/ SELL	SIZE	ENTRY PRICE	EXIT PRICE	CLOSE DATE /TIME	PROFIT/ LOSS

NOTES:	NEW BALANCE

ORDER DATE/TIME	TYPE	ORDER #	BUY/ SELL	SIZE	ENTRY PRICE	EXIT PRICE	CLOSE DATE /TIME	PROFIT/ LOSS

NOTES:	NEW BALANCE

ORDER DATE/TIME	TYPE	ORDER #	BUY/ SELL	SIZE	ENTRY PRICE	EXIT PRICE	CLOSE DATE /TIME	PROFIT/ LOSS

NOTES:	NEW BALANCE

ORDER DATE/TIME	TYPE	ORDER #	BUY/ SELL	SIZE	ENTRY PRICE	EXIT PRICE	CLOSE DATE /TIME	PROFIT/ LOSS

NOTES:	NEW BALANCE

ORDER DATE/TIME	TYPE	ORDER #	BUY/ SELL	SIZE	ENTRY PRICE	EXIT PRICE	CLOSE DATE /TIME	PROFIT/ LOSS

NOTES:	NEW BALANCE

TRADING LOG

ORDER DATE/TIME	TYPE	ORDER #	BUY/ SELL	SIZE	ENTRY PRICE	EXIT PRICE	CLOSE DATE /TIME	PROFIT/ LOSS

NOTES:					NEW BALANCE	

ORDER DATE/TIME	TYPE	ORDER #	BUY/ SELL	SIZE	ENTRY PRICE	EXIT PRICE	CLOSE DATE /TIME	PROFIT/ LOSS

NOTES:					NEW BALANCE	

ORDER DATE/TIME	TYPE	ORDER #	BUY/ SELL	SIZE	ENTRY PRICE	EXIT PRICE	CLOSE DATE /TIME	PROFIT/ LOSS

NOTES:					NEW BALANCE	

ORDER DATE/TIME	TYPE	ORDER #	BUY/ SELL	SIZE	ENTRY PRICE	EXIT PRICE	CLOSE DATE /TIME	PROFIT/ LOSS

NOTES:					NEW BALANCE	

ORDER DATE/TIME	TYPE	ORDER #	BUY/ SELL	SIZE	ENTRY PRICE	EXIT PRICE	CLOSE DATE /TIME	PROFIT/ LOSS

NOTES:					NEW BALANCE	

TRADING LOG

ORDER DATE/TIME	TYPE	ORDER #	BUY/SELL	SIZE	ENTRY PRICE	EXIT PRICE	CLOSE DATE /TIME	PROFIT/LOSS

NOTES:	NEW BALANCE

ORDER DATE/TIME	TYPE	ORDER #	BUY/SELL	SIZE	ENTRY PRICE	EXIT PRICE	CLOSE DATE /TIME	PROFIT/LOSS

NOTES:	NEW BALANCE

ORDER DATE/TIME	TYPE	ORDER #	BUY/SELL	SIZE	ENTRY PRICE	EXIT PRICE	CLOSE DATE /TIME	PROFIT/LOSS

NOTES:	NEW BALANCE

ORDER DATE/TIME	TYPE	ORDER #	BUY/SELL	SIZE	ENTRY PRICE	EXIT PRICE	CLOSE DATE /TIME	PROFIT/LOSS

NOTES:	NEW BALANCE

ORDER DATE/TIME	TYPE	ORDER #	BUY/SELL	SIZE	ENTRY PRICE	EXIT PRICE	CLOSE DATE /TIME	PROFIT/LOSS

NOTES:	NEW BALANCE

TRADING LOG

ORDER DATE/TIME	TYPE	ORDER #	BUY/ SELL	SIZE	ENTRY PRICE	EXIT PRICE	CLOSE DATE /TIME	PROFIT/ LOSS

NOTES:			NEW BALANCE

ORDER DATE/TIME	TYPE	ORDER #	BUY/ SELL	SIZE	ENTRY PRICE	EXIT PRICE	CLOSE DATE /TIME	PROFIT/ LOSS

NOTES:			NEW BALANCE

ORDER DATE/TIME	TYPE	ORDER #	BUY/ SELL	SIZE	ENTRY PRICE	EXIT PRICE	CLOSE DATE /TIME	PROFIT/ LOSS

NOTES:			NEW BALANCE

ORDER DATE/TIME	TYPE	ORDER #	BUY/ SELL	SIZE	ENTRY PRICE	EXIT PRICE	CLOSE DATE /TIME	PROFIT/ LOSS

NOTES:			NEW BALANCE

ORDER DATE/TIME	TYPE	ORDER #	BUY/ SELL	SIZE	ENTRY PRICE	EXIT PRICE	CLOSE DATE /TIME	PROFIT/ LOSS

NOTES:			NEW BALANCE

TRADING LOG

ORDER DATE/TIME	TYPE	ORDER #	BUY/ SELL	SIZE	ENTRY PRICE	EXIT PRICE	CLOSE DATE /TIME	PROFIT/ LOSS

NOTES:						NEW BALANCE

ORDER DATE/TIME	TYPE	ORDER #	BUY/ SELL	SIZE	ENTRY PRICE	EXIT PRICE	CLOSE DATE /TIME	PROFIT/ LOSS

NOTES:						NEW BALANCE

ORDER DATE/TIME	TYPE	ORDER #	BUY/ SELL	SIZE	ENTRY PRICE	EXIT PRICE	CLOSE DATE /TIME	PROFIT/ LOSS

NOTES:						NEW BALANCE

ORDER DATE/TIME	TYPE	ORDER #	BUY/ SELL	SIZE	ENTRY PRICE	EXIT PRICE	CLOSE DATE /TIME	PROFIT/ LOSS

NOTES:						NEW BALANCE

ORDER DATE/TIME	TYPE	ORDER #	BUY/ SELL	SIZE	ENTRY PRICE	EXIT PRICE	CLOSE DATE /TIME	PROFIT/ LOSS

NOTES:						NEW BALANCE

TRADING LOG

ORDER DATE/TIME	TYPE	ORDER #	BUY/ SELL	SIZE	ENTRY PRICE	EXIT PRICE	CLOSE DATE /TIME	PROFIT/ LOSS

NOTES:		NEW BALANCE

ORDER DATE/TIME	TYPE	ORDER #	BUY/ SELL	SIZE	ENTRY PRICE	EXIT PRICE	CLOSE DATE /TIME	PROFIT/ LOSS

NOTES:		NEW BALANCE

ORDER DATE/TIME	TYPE	ORDER #	BUY/ SELL	SIZE	ENTRY PRICE	EXIT PRICE	CLOSE DATE /TIME	PROFIT/ LOSS

NOTES:		NEW BALANCE

ORDER DATE/TIME	TYPE	ORDER #	BUY/ SELL	SIZE	ENTRY PRICE	EXIT PRICE	CLOSE DATE /TIME	PROFIT/ LOSS

NOTES:		NEW BALANCE

ORDER DATE/TIME	TYPE	ORDER #	BUY/ SELL	SIZE	ENTRY PRICE	EXIT PRICE	CLOSE DATE /TIME	PROFIT/ LOSS

NOTES:		NEW BALANCE

TRADING LOG

ORDER DATE/TIME	TYPE	ORDER #	BUY/ SELL	SIZE	ENTRY PRICE	EXIT PRICE	CLOSE DATE /TIME	PROFIT/ LOSS

NOTES:		NEW BALANCE

ORDER DATE/TIME	TYPE	ORDER #	BUY/ SELL	SIZE	ENTRY PRICE	EXIT PRICE	CLOSE DATE /TIME	PROFIT/ LOSS

NOTES:		NEW BALANCE

ORDER DATE/TIME	TYPE	ORDER #	BUY/ SELL	SIZE	ENTRY PRICE	EXIT PRICE	CLOSE DATE /TIME	PROFIT/ LOSS

NOTES:		NEW BALANCE

ORDER DATE/TIME	TYPE	ORDER #	BUY/ SELL	SIZE	ENTRY PRICE	EXIT PRICE	CLOSE DATE /TIME	PROFIT/ LOSS

NOTES:		NEW BALANCE

ORDER DATE/TIME	TYPE	ORDER #	BUY/ SELL	SIZE	ENTRY PRICE	EXIT PRICE	CLOSE DATE /TIME	PROFIT/ LOSS

NOTES:		NEW BALANCE

TRADING LOG

ORDER DATE/TIME	TYPE	ORDER #	BUY/ SELL	SIZE	ENTRY PRICE	EXIT PRICE	CLOSE DATE /TIME	PROFIT/ LOSS

NOTES:	NEW BALANCE

ORDER DATE/TIME	TYPE	ORDER #	BUY/ SELL	SIZE	ENTRY PRICE	EXIT PRICE	CLOSE DATE /TIME	PROFIT/ LOSS

NOTES:	NEW BALANCE

ORDER DATE/TIME	TYPE	ORDER #	BUY/ SELL	SIZE	ENTRY PRICE	EXIT PRICE	CLOSE DATE /TIME	PROFIT/ LOSS

NOTES:	NEW BALANCE

ORDER DATE/TIME	TYPE	ORDER #	BUY/ SELL	SIZE	ENTRY PRICE	EXIT PRICE	CLOSE DATE /TIME	PROFIT/ LOSS

NOTES:	NEW BALANCE

ORDER DATE/TIME	TYPE	ORDER #	BUY/ SELL	SIZE	ENTRY PRICE	EXIT PRICE	CLOSE DATE /TIME	PROFIT/ LOSS

NOTES:	NEW BALANCE

TRADING LOG

ORDER DATE/TIME	TYPE	ORDER #	BUY/SELL	SIZE	ENTRY PRICE	EXIT PRICE	CLOSE DATE /TIME	PROFIT/LOSS

NOTES:					NEW BALANCE	

ORDER DATE/TIME	TYPE	ORDER #	BUY/SELL	SIZE	ENTRY PRICE	EXIT PRICE	CLOSE DATE /TIME	PROFIT/LOSS

NOTES:					NEW BALANCE	

ORDER DATE/TIME	TYPE	ORDER #	BUY/SELL	SIZE	ENTRY PRICE	EXIT PRICE	CLOSE DATE /TIME	PROFIT/LOSS

NOTES:					NEW BALANCE	

ORDER DATE/TIME	TYPE	ORDER #	BUY/SELL	SIZE	ENTRY PRICE	EXIT PRICE	CLOSE DATE /TIME	PROFIT/LOSS

NOTES:					NEW BALANCE	

ORDER DATE/TIME	TYPE	ORDER #	BUY/SELL	SIZE	ENTRY PRICE	EXIT PRICE	CLOSE DATE /TIME	PROFIT/LOSS

NOTES:					NEW BALANCE	

TRADING LOG

ORDER DATE/TIME	TYPE	ORDER #	BUY/ SELL	SIZE	ENTRY PRICE	EXIT PRICE	CLOSE DATE /TIME	PROFIT/ LOSS

NOTES:		
	NEW BALANCE	

ORDER DATE/TIME	TYPE	ORDER #	BUY/ SELL	SIZE	ENTRY PRICE	EXIT PRICE	CLOSE DATE /TIME	PROFIT/ LOSS

NOTES:		
	NEW BALANCE	

ORDER DATE/TIME	TYPE	ORDER #	BUY/ SELL	SIZE	ENTRY PRICE	EXIT PRICE	CLOSE DATE /TIME	PROFIT/ LOSS

NOTES:		
	NEW BALANCE	

ORDER DATE/TIME	TYPE	ORDER #	BUY/ SELL	SIZE	ENTRY PRICE	EXIT PRICE	CLOSE DATE /TIME	PROFIT/ LOSS

NOTES:		
	NEW BALANCE	

ORDER DATE/TIME	TYPE	ORDER #	BUY/ SELL	SIZE	ENTRY PRICE	EXIT PRICE	CLOSE DATE /TIME	PROFIT/ LOSS

NOTES:		
	NEW BALANCE	

TRADING LOG

ORDER DATE/TIME	TYPE	ORDER #	BUY/ SELL	SIZE	ENTRY PRICE	EXIT PRICE	CLOSE DATE /TIME	PROFIT/ LOSS

NOTES:	NEW BALANCE

ORDER DATE/TIME	TYPE	ORDER #	BUY/ SELL	SIZE	ENTRY PRICE	EXIT PRICE	CLOSE DATE /TIME	PROFIT/ LOSS

NOTES:	NEW BALANCE

ORDER DATE/TIME	TYPE	ORDER #	BUY/ SELL	SIZE	ENTRY PRICE	EXIT PRICE	CLOSE DATE /TIME	PROFIT/ LOSS

NOTES:	NEW BALANCE

ORDER DATE/TIME	TYPE	ORDER #	BUY/ SELL	SIZE	ENTRY PRICE	EXIT PRICE	CLOSE DATE /TIME	PROFIT/ LOSS

NOTES:	NEW BALANCE

ORDER DATE/TIME	TYPE	ORDER #	BUY/ SELL	SIZE	ENTRY PRICE	EXIT PRICE	CLOSE DATE /TIME	PROFIT/ LOSS

NOTES:	NEW BALANCE

TRADING LOG

ORDER DATE/TIME	TYPE	ORDER #	BUY/ SELL	SIZE	ENTRY PRICE	EXIT PRICE	CLOSE DATE /TIME	PROFIT/ LOSS

NOTES:	NEW BALANCE

ORDER DATE/TIME	TYPE	ORDER #	BUY/ SELL	SIZE	ENTRY PRICE	EXIT PRICE	CLOSE DATE /TIME	PROFIT/ LOSS

NOTES:	NEW BALANCE

ORDER DATE/TIME	TYPE	ORDER #	BUY/ SELL	SIZE	ENTRY PRICE	EXIT PRICE	CLOSE DATE /TIME	PROFIT/ LOSS

NOTES:	NEW BALANCE

ORDER DATE/TIME	TYPE	ORDER #	BUY/ SELL	SIZE	ENTRY PRICE	EXIT PRICE	CLOSE DATE /TIME	PROFIT/ LOSS

NOTES:	NEW BALANCE

ORDER DATE/TIME	TYPE	ORDER #	BUY/ SELL	SIZE	ENTRY PRICE	EXIT PRICE	CLOSE DATE /TIME	PROFIT/ LOSS

NOTES:	NEW BALANCE

TRADING LOG

ORDER DATE/TIME	TYPE	ORDER #	BUY/ SELL	SIZE	ENTRY PRICE	EXIT PRICE	CLOSE DATE /TIME	PROFIT/ LOSS

NOTES:	NEW BALANCE

ORDER DATE/TIME	TYPE	ORDER #	BUY/ SELL	SIZE	ENTRY PRICE	EXIT PRICE	CLOSE DATE /TIME	PROFIT/ LOSS

NOTES:	NEW BALANCE

ORDER DATE/TIME	TYPE	ORDER #	BUY/ SELL	SIZE	ENTRY PRICE	EXIT PRICE	CLOSE DATE /TIME	PROFIT/ LOSS

NOTES:	NEW BALANCE

ORDER DATE/TIME	TYPE	ORDER #	BUY/ SELL	SIZE	ENTRY PRICE	EXIT PRICE	CLOSE DATE /TIME	PROFIT/ LOSS

NOTES:	NEW BALANCE

ORDER DATE/TIME	TYPE	ORDER #	BUY/ SELL	SIZE	ENTRY PRICE	EXIT PRICE	CLOSE DATE /TIME	PROFIT/ LOSS

NOTES:	NEW BALANCE

TRADING LOG

ORDER DATE/TIME	TYPE	ORDER #	BUY/ SELL	SIZE	ENTRY PRICE	EXIT PRICE	CLOSE DATE /TIME	PROFIT/ LOSS

NOTES:				NEW BALANCE	

ORDER DATE/TIME	TYPE	ORDER #	BUY/ SELL	SIZE	ENTRY PRICE	EXIT PRICE	CLOSE DATE /TIME	PROFIT/ LOSS

NOTES:				NEW BALANCE	

ORDER DATE/TIME	TYPE	ORDER #	BUY/ SELL	SIZE	ENTRY PRICE	EXIT PRICE	CLOSE DATE /TIME	PROFIT/ LOSS

NOTES:				NEW BALANCE	

ORDER DATE/TIME	TYPE	ORDER #	BUY/ SELL	SIZE	ENTRY PRICE	EXIT PRICE	CLOSE DATE /TIME	PROFIT/ LOSS

NOTES:				NEW BALANCE	

ORDER DATE/TIME	TYPE	ORDER #	BUY/ SELL	SIZE	ENTRY PRICE	EXIT PRICE	CLOSE DATE /TIME	PROFIT/ LOSS

NOTES:				NEW BALANCE	

TRADING LOG

ORDER DATE/TIME	TYPE	ORDER #	BUY/ SELL	SIZE	ENTRY PRICE	EXIT PRICE	CLOSE DATE /TIME	PROFIT/ LOSS

NOTES:	NEW BALANCE

ORDER DATE/TIME	TYPE	ORDER #	BUY/ SELL	SIZE	ENTRY PRICE	EXIT PRICE	CLOSE DATE /TIME	PROFIT/ LOSS

NOTES:	NEW BALANCE

ORDER DATE/TIME	TYPE	ORDER #	BUY/ SELL	SIZE	ENTRY PRICE	EXIT PRICE	CLOSE DATE /TIME	PROFIT/ LOSS

NOTES:	NEW BALANCE

ORDER DATE/TIME	TYPE	ORDER #	BUY/ SELL	SIZE	ENTRY PRICE	EXIT PRICE	CLOSE DATE /TIME	PROFIT/ LOSS

NOTES:	NEW BALANCE

ORDER DATE/TIME	TYPE	ORDER #	BUY/ SELL	SIZE	ENTRY PRICE	EXIT PRICE	CLOSE DATE /TIME	PROFIT/ LOSS

NOTES:	NEW BALANCE

TRADING LOG

ORDER DATE/TIME	TYPE	ORDER #	BUY/ SELL	SIZE	ENTRY PRICE	EXIT PRICE	CLOSE DATE /TIME	PROFIT/ LOSS

NOTES:			NEW BALANCE	

ORDER DATE/TIME	TYPE	ORDER #	BUY/ SELL	SIZE	ENTRY PRICE	EXIT PRICE	CLOSE DATE /TIME	PROFIT/ LOSS

NOTES:			NEW BALANCE	

ORDER DATE/TIME	TYPE	ORDER #	BUY/ SELL	SIZE	ENTRY PRICE	EXIT PRICE	CLOSE DATE /TIME	PROFIT/ LOSS

NOTES:			NEW BALANCE	

ORDER DATE/TIME	TYPE	ORDER #	BUY/ SELL	SIZE	ENTRY PRICE	EXIT PRICE	CLOSE DATE /TIME	PROFIT/ LOSS

NOTES:			NEW BALANCE	

ORDER DATE/TIME	TYPE	ORDER #	BUY/ SELL	SIZE	ENTRY PRICE	EXIT PRICE	CLOSE DATE /TIME	PROFIT/ LOSS

NOTES:			NEW BALANCE	

TRADING LOG

ORDER DATE/TIME	TYPE	ORDER #	BUY/SELL	SIZE	ENTRY PRICE	EXIT PRICE	CLOSE DATE /TIME	PROFIT/LOSS

NOTES:							NEW BALANCE	

ORDER DATE/TIME	TYPE	ORDER #	BUY/SELL	SIZE	ENTRY PRICE	EXIT PRICE	CLOSE DATE /TIME	PROFIT/LOSS

NOTES:							NEW BALANCE	

ORDER DATE/TIME	TYPE	ORDER #	BUY/SELL	SIZE	ENTRY PRICE	EXIT PRICE	CLOSE DATE /TIME	PROFIT/LOSS

NOTES:							NEW BALANCE	

ORDER DATE/TIME	TYPE	ORDER #	BUY/SELL	SIZE	ENTRY PRICE	EXIT PRICE	CLOSE DATE /TIME	PROFIT/LOSS

NOTES:							NEW BALANCE	

ORDER DATE/TIME	TYPE	ORDER #	BUY/SELL	SIZE	ENTRY PRICE	EXIT PRICE	CLOSE DATE /TIME	PROFIT/LOSS

NOTES:							NEW BALANCE	

TRADING LOG

ORDER DATE/TIME	TYPE	ORDER #	BUY/ SELL	SIZE	ENTRY PRICE	EXIT PRICE	CLOSE DATE /TIME	PROFIT/ LOSS

NOTES:						NEW BALANCE		

ORDER DATE/TIME	TYPE	ORDER #	BUY/ SELL	SIZE	ENTRY PRICE	EXIT PRICE	CLOSE DATE /TIME	PROFIT/ LOSS

NOTES:						NEW BALANCE		

ORDER DATE/TIME	TYPE	ORDER #	BUY/ SELL	SIZE	ENTRY PRICE	EXIT PRICE	CLOSE DATE /TIME	PROFIT/ LOSS

NOTES:						NEW BALANCE		

ORDER DATE/TIME	TYPE	ORDER #	BUY/ SELL	SIZE	ENTRY PRICE	EXIT PRICE	CLOSE DATE /TIME	PROFIT/ LOSS

NOTES:						NEW BALANCE		

ORDER DATE/TIME	TYPE	ORDER #	BUY/ SELL	SIZE	ENTRY PRICE	EXIT PRICE	CLOSE DATE /TIME	PROFIT/ LOSS

NOTES:						NEW BALANCE		

TRADING LOG

ORDER DATE/TIME	TYPE	ORDER #	BUY/ SELL	SIZE	ENTRY PRICE	EXIT PRICE	CLOSE DATE /TIME	PROFIT/ LOSS

NOTES:	NEW BALANCE

ORDER DATE/TIME	TYPE	ORDER #	BUY/ SELL	SIZE	ENTRY PRICE	EXIT PRICE	CLOSE DATE /TIME	PROFIT/ LOSS

NOTES:	NEW BALANCE

ORDER DATE/TIME	TYPE	ORDER #	BUY/ SELL	SIZE	ENTRY PRICE	EXIT PRICE	CLOSE DATE /TIME	PROFIT/ LOSS

NOTES:	NEW BALANCE

ORDER DATE/TIME	TYPE	ORDER #	BUY/ SELL	SIZE	ENTRY PRICE	EXIT PRICE	CLOSE DATE /TIME	PROFIT/ LOSS

NOTES:	NEW BALANCE

ORDER DATE/TIME	TYPE	ORDER #	BUY/ SELL	SIZE	ENTRY PRICE	EXIT PRICE	CLOSE DATE /TIME	PROFIT/ LOSS

NOTES:	NEW BALANCE

TRADING LOG

ORDER DATE/TIME	TYPE	ORDER #	BUY/ SELL	SIZE	ENTRY PRICE	EXIT PRICE	CLOSE DATE /TIME	PROFIT/ LOSS

NOTES:	NEW BALANCE

ORDER DATE/TIME	TYPE	ORDER #	BUY/ SELL	SIZE	ENTRY PRICE	EXIT PRICE	CLOSE DATE /TIME	PROFIT/ LOSS

NOTES:	NEW BALANCE

ORDER DATE/TIME	TYPE	ORDER #	BUY/ SELL	SIZE	ENTRY PRICE	EXIT PRICE	CLOSE DATE /TIME	PROFIT/ LOSS

NOTES:	NEW BALANCE

ORDER DATE/TIME	TYPE	ORDER #	BUY/ SELL	SIZE	ENTRY PRICE	EXIT PRICE	CLOSE DATE /TIME	PROFIT/ LOSS

NOTES:	NEW BALANCE

ORDER DATE/TIME	TYPE	ORDER #	BUY/ SELL	SIZE	ENTRY PRICE	EXIT PRICE	CLOSE DATE /TIME	PROFIT/ LOSS

NOTES:	NEW BALANCE

TRADING LOG

ORDER DATE/TIME	TYPE	ORDER #	BUY/ SELL	SIZE	ENTRY PRICE	EXIT PRICE	CLOSE DATE /TIME	PROFIT/ LOSS

NOTES:						NEW BALANCE	

ORDER DATE/TIME	TYPE	ORDER #	BUY/ SELL	SIZE	ENTRY PRICE	EXIT PRICE	CLOSE DATE /TIME	PROFIT/ LOSS

NOTES:						NEW BALANCE	

ORDER DATE/TIME	TYPE	ORDER #	BUY/ SELL	SIZE	ENTRY PRICE	EXIT PRICE	CLOSE DATE /TIME	PROFIT/ LOSS

NOTES:						NEW BALANCE	

ORDER DATE/TIME	TYPE	ORDER #	BUY/ SELL	SIZE	ENTRY PRICE	EXIT PRICE	CLOSE DATE /TIME	PROFIT/ LOSS

NOTES:						NEW BALANCE	

ORDER DATE/TIME	TYPE	ORDER #	BUY/ SELL	SIZE	ENTRY PRICE	EXIT PRICE	CLOSE DATE /TIME	PROFIT/ LOSS

NOTES:						NEW BALANCE	

TRADING LOG

ORDER DATE/TIME	TYPE	ORDER #	BUY/SELL	SIZE	ENTRY PRICE	EXIT PRICE	CLOSE DATE /TIME	PROFIT/LOSS

NOTES:	NEW BALANCE

ORDER DATE/TIME	TYPE	ORDER #	BUY/SELL	SIZE	ENTRY PRICE	EXIT PRICE	CLOSE DATE /TIME	PROFIT/LOSS

NOTES:	NEW BALANCE

ORDER DATE/TIME	TYPE	ORDER #	BUY/SELL	SIZE	ENTRY PRICE	EXIT PRICE	CLOSE DATE /TIME	PROFIT/LOSS

NOTES:	NEW BALANCE

ORDER DATE/TIME	TYPE	ORDER #	BUY/SELL	SIZE	ENTRY PRICE	EXIT PRICE	CLOSE DATE /TIME	PROFIT/LOSS

NOTES:	NEW BALANCE

ORDER DATE/TIME	TYPE	ORDER #	BUY/SELL	SIZE	ENTRY PRICE	EXIT PRICE	CLOSE DATE /TIME	PROFIT/LOSS

NOTES:	NEW BALANCE

TRADING LOG

ORDER DATE/TIME	TYPE	ORDER #	BUY/SELL	SIZE	ENTRY PRICE	EXIT PRICE	CLOSE DATE /TIME	PROFIT/ LOSS

NOTES:	NEW BALANCE

ORDER DATE/TIME	TYPE	ORDER #	BUY/SELL	SIZE	ENTRY PRICE	EXIT PRICE	CLOSE DATE /TIME	PROFIT/ LOSS

NOTES:	NEW BALANCE

ORDER DATE/TIME	TYPE	ORDER #	BUY/SELL	SIZE	ENTRY PRICE	EXIT PRICE	CLOSE DATE /TIME	PROFIT/ LOSS

NOTES:	NEW BALANCE

ORDER DATE/TIME	TYPE	ORDER #	BUY/SELL	SIZE	ENTRY PRICE	EXIT PRICE	CLOSE DATE /TIME	PROFIT/ LOSS

NOTES:	NEW BALANCE

ORDER DATE/TIME	TYPE	ORDER #	BUY/SELL	SIZE	ENTRY PRICE	EXIT PRICE	CLOSE DATE /TIME	PROFIT/ LOSS

NOTES:	NEW BALANCE

TRADING LOG

ORDER DATE/TIME	TYPE	ORDER #	BUY/ SELL	SIZE	ENTRY PRICE	EXIT PRICE	CLOSE DATE /TIME	PROFIT/ LOSS

NOTES:		NEW BALANCE

ORDER DATE/TIME	TYPE	ORDER #	BUY/ SELL	SIZE	ENTRY PRICE	EXIT PRICE	CLOSE DATE /TIME	PROFIT/ LOSS

NOTES:		NEW BALANCE

ORDER DATE/TIME	TYPE	ORDER #	BUY/ SELL	SIZE	ENTRY PRICE	EXIT PRICE	CLOSE DATE /TIME	PROFIT/ LOSS

NOTES:		NEW BALANCE

ORDER DATE/TIME	TYPE	ORDER #	BUY/ SELL	SIZE	ENTRY PRICE	EXIT PRICE	CLOSE DATE /TIME	PROFIT/ LOSS

NOTES:		NEW BALANCE

ORDER DATE/TIME	TYPE	ORDER #	BUY/ SELL	SIZE	ENTRY PRICE	EXIT PRICE	CLOSE DATE /TIME	PROFIT/ LOSS

NOTES:		NEW BALANCE

TRADING LOG

ORDER DATE/TIME	TYPE	ORDER #	BUY/ SELL	SIZE	ENTRY PRICE	EXIT PRICE	CLOSE DATE /TIME	PROFIT/ LOSS

NOTES:	NEW BALANCE

ORDER DATE/TIME	TYPE	ORDER #	BUY/ SELL	SIZE	ENTRY PRICE	EXIT PRICE	CLOSE DATE /TIME	PROFIT/ LOSS

NOTES:	NEW BALANCE

ORDER DATE/TIME	TYPE	ORDER #	BUY/ SELL	SIZE	ENTRY PRICE	EXIT PRICE	CLOSE DATE /TIME	PROFIT/ LOSS

NOTES:	NEW BALANCE

ORDER DATE/TIME	TYPE	ORDER #	BUY/ SELL	SIZE	ENTRY PRICE	EXIT PRICE	CLOSE DATE /TIME	PROFIT/ LOSS

NOTES:	NEW BALANCE

ORDER DATE/TIME	TYPE	ORDER #	BUY/ SELL	SIZE	ENTRY PRICE	EXIT PRICE	CLOSE DATE /TIME	PROFIT/ LOSS

NOTES:	NEW BALANCE

TRADING LOG

ORDER DATE/TIME	TYPE	ORDER #	BUY/ SELL	SIZE	ENTRY PRICE	EXIT PRICE	CLOSE DATE /TIME	PROFIT/ LOSS

NOTES:	NEW BALANCE

ORDER DATE/TIME	TYPE	ORDER #	BUY/ SELL	SIZE	ENTRY PRICE	EXIT PRICE	CLOSE DATE /TIME	PROFIT/ LOSS

NOTES:	NEW BALANCE

ORDER DATE/TIME	TYPE	ORDER #	BUY/ SELL	SIZE	ENTRY PRICE	EXIT PRICE	CLOSE DATE /TIME	PROFIT/ LOSS

NOTES:	NEW BALANCE

ORDER DATE/TIME	TYPE	ORDER #	BUY/ SELL	SIZE	ENTRY PRICE	EXIT PRICE	CLOSE DATE /TIME	PROFIT/ LOSS

NOTES:	NEW BALANCE

ORDER DATE/TIME	TYPE	ORDER #	BUY/ SELL	SIZE	ENTRY PRICE	EXIT PRICE	CLOSE DATE /TIME	PROFIT/ LOSS

NOTES:	NEW BALANCE

TRADING LOG

ORDER DATE/TIME	TYPE	ORDER #	BUY/SELL	SIZE	ENTRY PRICE	EXIT PRICE	CLOSE DATE /TIME	PROFIT/LOSS

NOTES:	NEW BALANCE

ORDER DATE/TIME	TYPE	ORDER #	BUY/SELL	SIZE	ENTRY PRICE	EXIT PRICE	CLOSE DATE /TIME	PROFIT/LOSS

NOTES:	NEW BALANCE

ORDER DATE/TIME	TYPE	ORDER #	BUY/SELL	SIZE	ENTRY PRICE	EXIT PRICE	CLOSE DATE /TIME	PROFIT/LOSS

NOTES:	NEW BALANCE

ORDER DATE/TIME	TYPE	ORDER #	BUY/SELL	SIZE	ENTRY PRICE	EXIT PRICE	CLOSE DATE /TIME	PROFIT/LOSS

NOTES:	NEW BALANCE

ORDER DATE/TIME	TYPE	ORDER #	BUY/SELL	SIZE	ENTRY PRICE	EXIT PRICE	CLOSE DATE /TIME	PROFIT/LOSS

NOTES:	NEW BALANCE

TRADING LOG

ORDER DATE/TIME	TYPE	ORDER #	BUY/ SELL	SIZE	ENTRY PRICE	EXIT PRICE	CLOSE DATE /TIME	PROFIT/ LOSS

NOTES:	
	NEW BALANCE

ORDER DATE/TIME	TYPE	ORDER #	BUY/ SELL	SIZE	ENTRY PRICE	EXIT PRICE	CLOSE DATE /TIME	PROFIT/ LOSS

NOTES:	
	NEW BALANCE

ORDER DATE/TIME	TYPE	ORDER #	BUY/ SELL	SIZE	ENTRY PRICE	EXIT PRICE	CLOSE DATE /TIME	PROFIT/ LOSS

NOTES:	
	NEW BALANCE

ORDER DATE/TIME	TYPE	ORDER #	BUY/ SELL	SIZE	ENTRY PRICE	EXIT PRICE	CLOSE DATE /TIME	PROFIT/ LOSS

NOTES:	
	NEW BALANCE

ORDER DATE/TIME	TYPE	ORDER #	BUY/ SELL	SIZE	ENTRY PRICE	EXIT PRICE	CLOSE DATE /TIME	PROFIT/ LOSS

NOTES:	
	NEW BALANCE

TRADING LOG

ORDER DATE/TIME	TYPE	ORDER #	BUY/ SELL	SIZE	ENTRY PRICE	EXIT PRICE	CLOSE DATE /TIME	PROFIT/ LOSS

NOTES:	NEW BALANCE

ORDER DATE/TIME	TYPE	ORDER #	BUY/ SELL	SIZE	ENTRY PRICE	EXIT PRICE	CLOSE DATE /TIME	PROFIT/ LOSS

NOTES:	NEW BALANCE

ORDER DATE/TIME	TYPE	ORDER #	BUY/ SELL	SIZE	ENTRY PRICE	EXIT PRICE	CLOSE DATE /TIME	PROFIT/ LOSS

NOTES:	NEW BALANCE

ORDER DATE/TIME	TYPE	ORDER #	BUY/ SELL	SIZE	ENTRY PRICE	EXIT PRICE	CLOSE DATE /TIME	PROFIT/ LOSS

NOTES:	NEW BALANCE

ORDER DATE/TIME	TYPE	ORDER #	BUY/ SELL	SIZE	ENTRY PRICE	EXIT PRICE	CLOSE DATE /TIME	PROFIT/ LOSS

NOTES:	NEW BALANCE

TRADING LOG

ORDER DATE/TIME	TYPE	ORDER #	BUY/ SELL	SIZE	ENTRY PRICE	EXIT PRICE	CLOSE DATE /TIME	PROFIT/ LOSS

NOTES:	NEW BALANCE

ORDER DATE/TIME	TYPE	ORDER #	BUY/ SELL	SIZE	ENTRY PRICE	EXIT PRICE	CLOSE DATE /TIME	PROFIT/ LOSS

NOTES:	NEW BALANCE

ORDER DATE/TIME	TYPE	ORDER #	BUY/ SELL	SIZE	ENTRY PRICE	EXIT PRICE	CLOSE DATE /TIME	PROFIT/ LOSS

NOTES:	NEW BALANCE

ORDER DATE/TIME	TYPE	ORDER #	BUY/ SELL	SIZE	ENTRY PRICE	EXIT PRICE	CLOSE DATE /TIME	PROFIT/ LOSS

NOTES:	NEW BALANCE

ORDER DATE/TIME	TYPE	ORDER #	BUY/ SELL	SIZE	ENTRY PRICE	EXIT PRICE	CLOSE DATE /TIME	PROFIT/ LOSS

NOTES:	NEW BALANCE

TRADING LOG

ORDER DATE/TIME	TYPE	ORDER #	BUY/ SELL	SIZE	ENTRY PRICE	EXIT PRICE	CLOSE DATE /TIME	PROFIT/ LOSS

NOTES:	NEW BALANCE

ORDER DATE/TIME	TYPE	ORDER #	BUY/ SELL	SIZE	ENTRY PRICE	EXIT PRICE	CLOSE DATE /TIME	PROFIT/ LOSS

NOTES:	NEW BALANCE

ORDER DATE/TIME	TYPE	ORDER #	BUY/ SELL	SIZE	ENTRY PRICE	EXIT PRICE	CLOSE DATE /TIME	PROFIT/ LOSS

NOTES:	NEW BALANCE

ORDER DATE/TIME	TYPE	ORDER #	BUY/ SELL	SIZE	ENTRY PRICE	EXIT PRICE	CLOSE DATE /TIME	PROFIT/ LOSS

NOTES:	NEW BALANCE

ORDER DATE/TIME	TYPE	ORDER #	BUY/ SELL	SIZE	ENTRY PRICE	EXIT PRICE	CLOSE DATE /TIME	PROFIT/ LOSS

NOTES:	NEW BALANCE

TRADING LOG

ORDER DATE/TIME	TYPE	ORDER #	BUY/ SELL	SIZE	ENTRY PRICE	EXIT PRICE	CLOSE DATE /TIME	PROFIT/ LOSS

NOTES:	NEW BALANCE

ORDER DATE/TIME	TYPE	ORDER #	BUY/ SELL	SIZE	ENTRY PRICE	EXIT PRICE	CLOSE DATE /TIME	PROFIT/ LOSS

NOTES:	NEW BALANCE

ORDER DATE/TIME	TYPE	ORDER #	BUY/ SELL	SIZE	ENTRY PRICE	EXIT PRICE	CLOSE DATE /TIME	PROFIT/ LOSS

NOTES:	NEW BALANCE

ORDER DATE/TIME	TYPE	ORDER #	BUY/ SELL	SIZE	ENTRY PRICE	EXIT PRICE	CLOSE DATE /TIME	PROFIT/ LOSS

NOTES:	NEW BALANCE

ORDER DATE/TIME	TYPE	ORDER #	BUY/ SELL	SIZE	ENTRY PRICE	EXIT PRICE	CLOSE DATE /TIME	PROFIT/ LOSS

NOTES:	NEW BALANCE

TRADING LOG

ORDER DATE/TIME	TYPE	ORDER #	BUY/ SELL	SIZE	ENTRY PRICE	EXIT PRICE	CLOSE DATE /TIME	PROFIT/ LOSS

NOTES:	NEW BALANCE

ORDER DATE/TIME	TYPE	ORDER #	BUY/ SELL	SIZE	ENTRY PRICE	EXIT PRICE	CLOSE DATE /TIME	PROFIT/ LOSS

NOTES:	NEW BALANCE

ORDER DATE/TIME	TYPE	ORDER #	BUY/ SELL	SIZE	ENTRY PRICE	EXIT PRICE	CLOSE DATE /TIME	PROFIT/ LOSS

NOTES:	NEW BALANCE

ORDER DATE/TIME	TYPE	ORDER #	BUY/ SELL	SIZE	ENTRY PRICE	EXIT PRICE	CLOSE DATE /TIME	PROFIT/ LOSS

NOTES:	NEW BALANCE

ORDER DATE/TIME	TYPE	ORDER #	BUY/ SELL	SIZE	ENTRY PRICE	EXIT PRICE	CLOSE DATE /TIME	PROFIT/ LOSS

NOTES:	NEW BALANCE

TRADING LOG

ORDER DATE/TIME	TYPE	ORDER #	BUY/ SELL	SIZE	ENTRY PRICE	EXIT PRICE	CLOSE DATE /TIME	PROFIT/ LOSS

NOTES:	NEW BALANCE

ORDER DATE/TIME	TYPE	ORDER #	BUY/ SELL	SIZE	ENTRY PRICE	EXIT PRICE	CLOSE DATE /TIME	PROFIT/ LOSS

NOTES:	NEW BALANCE

ORDER DATE/TIME	TYPE	ORDER #	BUY/ SELL	SIZE	ENTRY PRICE	EXIT PRICE	CLOSE DATE /TIME	PROFIT/ LOSS

NOTES:	NEW BALANCE

ORDER DATE/TIME	TYPE	ORDER #	BUY/ SELL	SIZE	ENTRY PRICE	EXIT PRICE	CLOSE DATE /TIME	PROFIT/ LOSS

NOTES:	NEW BALANCE

ORDER DATE/TIME	TYPE	ORDER #	BUY/ SELL	SIZE	ENTRY PRICE	EXIT PRICE	CLOSE DATE /TIME	PROFIT/ LOSS

NOTES:	NEW BALANCE

TRADING LOG

ORDER DATE/TIME	TYPE	ORDER #	BUY/ SELL	SIZE	ENTRY PRICE	EXIT PRICE	CLOSE DATE /TIME	PROFIT/ LOSS

NOTES:	NEW BALANCE

ORDER DATE/TIME	TYPE	ORDER #	BUY/ SELL	SIZE	ENTRY PRICE	EXIT PRICE	CLOSE DATE /TIME	PROFIT/ LOSS

NOTES:	NEW BALANCE

ORDER DATE/TIME	TYPE	ORDER #	BUY/ SELL	SIZE	ENTRY PRICE	EXIT PRICE	CLOSE DATE /TIME	PROFIT/ LOSS

NOTES:	NEW BALANCE

ORDER DATE/TIME	TYPE	ORDER #	BUY/ SELL	SIZE	ENTRY PRICE	EXIT PRICE	CLOSE DATE /TIME	PROFIT/ LOSS

NOTES:	NEW BALANCE

ORDER DATE/TIME	TYPE	ORDER #	BUY/ SELL	SIZE	ENTRY PRICE	EXIT PRICE	CLOSE DATE /TIME	PROFIT/ LOSS

NOTES:	NEW BALANCE

TRADING LOG

ORDER DATE/TIME	TYPE	ORDER #	BUY/ SELL	SIZE	ENTRY PRICE	EXIT PRICE	CLOSE DATE /TIME	PROFIT/ LOSS

NOTES:		NEW BALANCE

ORDER DATE/TIME	TYPE	ORDER #	BUY/ SELL	SIZE	ENTRY PRICE	EXIT PRICE	CLOSE DATE /TIME	PROFIT/ LOSS

NOTES:		NEW BALANCE

ORDER DATE/TIME	TYPE	ORDER #	BUY/ SELL	SIZE	ENTRY PRICE	EXIT PRICE	CLOSE DATE /TIME	PROFIT/ LOSS

NOTES:		NEW BALANCE

ORDER DATE/TIME	TYPE	ORDER #	BUY/ SELL	SIZE	ENTRY PRICE	EXIT PRICE	CLOSE DATE /TIME	PROFIT/ LOSS

NOTES:		NEW BALANCE

ORDER DATE/TIME	TYPE	ORDER #	BUY/ SELL	SIZE	ENTRY PRICE	EXIT PRICE	CLOSE DATE /TIME	PROFIT/ LOSS

NOTES:		NEW BALANCE

TRADING LOG

ORDER DATE/TIME	TYPE	ORDER #	BUY/ SELL	SIZE	ENTRY PRICE	EXIT PRICE	CLOSE DATE /TIME	PROFIT/ LOSS

NOTES:	NEW BALANCE

ORDER DATE/TIME	TYPE	ORDER #	BUY/ SELL	SIZE	ENTRY PRICE	EXIT PRICE	CLOSE DATE /TIME	PROFIT/ LOSS

NOTES:	NEW BALANCE

ORDER DATE/TIME	TYPE	ORDER #	BUY/ SELL	SIZE	ENTRY PRICE	EXIT PRICE	CLOSE DATE /TIME	PROFIT/ LOSS

NOTES:	NEW BALANCE

ORDER DATE/TIME	TYPE	ORDER #	BUY/ SELL	SIZE	ENTRY PRICE	EXIT PRICE	CLOSE DATE /TIME	PROFIT/ LOSS

NOTES:	NEW BALANCE

ORDER DATE/TIME	TYPE	ORDER #	BUY/ SELL	SIZE	ENTRY PRICE	EXIT PRICE	CLOSE DATE /TIME	PROFIT/ LOSS

NOTES:	NEW BALANCE

TRADING LOG

ORDER DATE/TIME	TYPE	ORDER #	BUY/ SELL	SIZE	ENTRY PRICE	EXIT PRICE	CLOSE DATE /TIME	PROFIT/ LOSS

NOTES:	NEW BALANCE

ORDER DATE/TIME	TYPE	ORDER #	BUY/ SELL	SIZE	ENTRY PRICE	EXIT PRICE	CLOSE DATE /TIME	PROFIT/ LOSS

NOTES:	NEW BALANCE

ORDER DATE/TIME	TYPE	ORDER #	BUY/ SELL	SIZE	ENTRY PRICE	EXIT PRICE	CLOSE DATE /TIME	PROFIT/ LOSS

NOTES:	NEW BALANCE

ORDER DATE/TIME	TYPE	ORDER #	BUY/ SELL	SIZE	ENTRY PRICE	EXIT PRICE	CLOSE DATE /TIME	PROFIT/ LOSS

NOTES:	NEW BALANCE

ORDER DATE/TIME	TYPE	ORDER #	BUY/ SELL	SIZE	ENTRY PRICE	EXIT PRICE	CLOSE DATE /TIME	PROFIT/ LOSS

NOTES:	NEW BALANCE

TRADING LOG

ORDER DATE/TIME	TYPE	ORDER #	BUY/ SELL	SIZE	ENTRY PRICE	EXIT PRICE	CLOSE DATE /TIME	PROFIT/ LOSS

NOTES:	NEW BALANCE

ORDER DATE/TIME	TYPE	ORDER #	BUY/ SELL	SIZE	ENTRY PRICE	EXIT PRICE	CLOSE DATE /TIME	PROFIT/ LOSS

NOTES:	NEW BALANCE

ORDER DATE/TIME	TYPE	ORDER #	BUY/ SELL	SIZE	ENTRY PRICE	EXIT PRICE	CLOSE DATE /TIME	PROFIT/ LOSS

NOTES:	NEW BALANCE

ORDER DATE/TIME	TYPE	ORDER #	BUY/ SELL	SIZE	ENTRY PRICE	EXIT PRICE	CLOSE DATE /TIME	PROFIT/ LOSS

NOTES:	NEW BALANCE

ORDER DATE/TIME	TYPE	ORDER #	BUY/ SELL	SIZE	ENTRY PRICE	EXIT PRICE	CLOSE DATE /TIME	PROFIT/ LOSS

NOTES:	NEW BALANCE

TRADING LOG

ORDER DATE/TIME	TYPE	ORDER #	BUY/ SELL	SIZE	ENTRY PRICE	EXIT PRICE	CLOSE DATE /TIME	PROFIT/ LOSS

NOTES:	
	NEW BALANCE

ORDER DATE/TIME	TYPE	ORDER #	BUY/ SELL	SIZE	ENTRY PRICE	EXIT PRICE	CLOSE DATE /TIME	PROFIT/ LOSS

NOTES:	
	NEW BALANCE

ORDER DATE/TIME	TYPE	ORDER #	BUY/ SELL	SIZE	ENTRY PRICE	EXIT PRICE	CLOSE DATE /TIME	PROFIT/ LOSS

NOTES:	
	NEW BALANCE

ORDER DATE/TIME	TYPE	ORDER #	BUY/ SELL	SIZE	ENTRY PRICE	EXIT PRICE	CLOSE DATE /TIME	PROFIT/ LOSS

NOTES:	
	NEW BALANCE

ORDER DATE/TIME	TYPE	ORDER #	BUY/ SELL	SIZE	ENTRY PRICE	EXIT PRICE	CLOSE DATE /TIME	PROFIT/ LOSS

NOTES:	
	NEW BALANCE

TRADING LOG

ORDER DATE/TIME	TYPE	ORDER #	BUY/ SELL	SIZE	ENTRY PRICE	EXIT PRICE	CLOSE DATE /TIME	PROFIT/ LOSS

NOTES:	NEW BALANCE

ORDER DATE/TIME	TYPE	ORDER #	BUY/ SELL	SIZE	ENTRY PRICE	EXIT PRICE	CLOSE DATE /TIME	PROFIT/ LOSS

NOTES:	NEW BALANCE

ORDER DATE/TIME	TYPE	ORDER #	BUY/ SELL	SIZE	ENTRY PRICE	EXIT PRICE	CLOSE DATE /TIME	PROFIT/ LOSS

NOTES:	NEW BALANCE

ORDER DATE/TIME	TYPE	ORDER #	BUY/ SELL	SIZE	ENTRY PRICE	EXIT PRICE	CLOSE DATE /TIME	PROFIT/ LOSS

NOTES:	NEW BALANCE

ORDER DATE/TIME	TYPE	ORDER #	BUY/ SELL	SIZE	ENTRY PRICE	EXIT PRICE	CLOSE DATE /TIME	PROFIT/ LOSS

NOTES:	NEW BALANCE

TRADING LOG

ORDER DATE/TIME	TYPE	ORDER #	BUY/ SELL	SIZE	ENTRY PRICE	EXIT PRICE	CLOSE DATE /TIME	PROFIT/ LOSS

NOTES:			NEW BALANCE

ORDER DATE/TIME	TYPE	ORDER #	BUY/ SELL	SIZE	ENTRY PRICE	EXIT PRICE	CLOSE DATE /TIME	PROFIT/ LOSS

NOTES:			NEW BALANCE

ORDER DATE/TIME	TYPE	ORDER #	BUY/ SELL	SIZE	ENTRY PRICE	EXIT PRICE	CLOSE DATE /TIME	PROFIT/ LOSS

NOTES:			NEW BALANCE

ORDER DATE/TIME	TYPE	ORDER #	BUY/ SELL	SIZE	ENTRY PRICE	EXIT PRICE	CLOSE DATE /TIME	PROFIT/ LOSS

NOTES:			NEW BALANCE

ORDER DATE/TIME	TYPE	ORDER #	BUY/ SELL	SIZE	ENTRY PRICE	EXIT PRICE	CLOSE DATE /TIME	PROFIT/ LOSS

NOTES:			NEW BALANCE

TRADING LOG

ORDER DATE/TIME	TYPE	ORDER #	BUY/SELL	SIZE	ENTRY PRICE	EXIT PRICE	CLOSE DATE /TIME	PROFIT/LOSS

NOTES:			NEW BALANCE

ORDER DATE/TIME	TYPE	ORDER #	BUY/SELL	SIZE	ENTRY PRICE	EXIT PRICE	CLOSE DATE /TIME	PROFIT/LOSS

NOTES:			NEW BALANCE

ORDER DATE/TIME	TYPE	ORDER #	BUY/SELL	SIZE	ENTRY PRICE	EXIT PRICE	CLOSE DATE /TIME	PROFIT/LOSS

NOTES:			NEW BALANCE

ORDER DATE/TIME	TYPE	ORDER #	BUY/SELL	SIZE	ENTRY PRICE	EXIT PRICE	CLOSE DATE /TIME	PROFIT/LOSS

NOTES:			NEW BALANCE

ORDER DATE/TIME	TYPE	ORDER #	BUY/SELL	SIZE	ENTRY PRICE	EXIT PRICE	CLOSE DATE /TIME	PROFIT/LOSS

NOTES:			NEW BALANCE

TRADING LOG

ORDER DATE/TIME	TYPE	ORDER #	BUY/ SELL	SIZE	ENTRY PRICE	EXIT PRICE	CLOSE DATE /TIME	PROFIT/ LOSS

NOTES:	NEW BALANCE

ORDER DATE/TIME	TYPE	ORDER #	BUY/ SELL	SIZE	ENTRY PRICE	EXIT PRICE	CLOSE DATE /TIME	PROFIT/ LOSS

NOTES:	NEW BALANCE

ORDER DATE/TIME	TYPE	ORDER #	BUY/ SELL	SIZE	ENTRY PRICE	EXIT PRICE	CLOSE DATE /TIME	PROFIT/ LOSS

NOTES:	NEW BALANCE

ORDER DATE/TIME	TYPE	ORDER #	BUY/ SELL	SIZE	ENTRY PRICE	EXIT PRICE	CLOSE DATE /TIME	PROFIT/ LOSS

NOTES:	NEW BALANCE

ORDER DATE/TIME	TYPE	ORDER #	BUY/ SELL	SIZE	ENTRY PRICE	EXIT PRICE	CLOSE DATE /TIME	PROFIT/ LOSS

NOTES:	NEW BALANCE

TRADING LOG

ORDER DATE/TIME	TYPE	ORDER #	BUY/ SELL	SIZE	ENTRY PRICE	EXIT PRICE	CLOSE DATE /TIME	PROFIT/ LOSS

NOTES:	NEW BALANCE

ORDER DATE/TIME	TYPE	ORDER #	BUY/ SELL	SIZE	ENTRY PRICE	EXIT PRICE	CLOSE DATE /TIME	PROFIT/ LOSS

NOTES:	NEW BALANCE

ORDER DATE/TIME	TYPE	ORDER #	BUY/ SELL	SIZE	ENTRY PRICE	EXIT PRICE	CLOSE DATE /TIME	PROFIT/ LOSS

NOTES:	NEW BALANCE

ORDER DATE/TIME	TYPE	ORDER #	BUY/ SELL	SIZE	ENTRY PRICE	EXIT PRICE	CLOSE DATE /TIME	PROFIT/ LOSS

NOTES:	NEW BALANCE

ORDER DATE/TIME	TYPE	ORDER #	BUY/ SELL	SIZE	ENTRY PRICE	EXIT PRICE	CLOSE DATE /TIME	PROFIT/ LOSS

NOTES:	NEW BALANCE

TRADING LOG

ORDER DATE/TIME	TYPE	ORDER #	BUY/SELL	SIZE	ENTRY PRICE	EXIT PRICE	CLOSE DATE /TIME	PROFIT/LOSS

NOTES:		NEW BALANCE

ORDER DATE/TIME	TYPE	ORDER #	BUY/SELL	SIZE	ENTRY PRICE	EXIT PRICE	CLOSE DATE /TIME	PROFIT/LOSS

NOTES:		NEW BALANCE

ORDER DATE/TIME	TYPE	ORDER #	BUY/SELL	SIZE	ENTRY PRICE	EXIT PRICE	CLOSE DATE /TIME	PROFIT/LOSS

NOTES:		NEW BALANCE

ORDER DATE/TIME	TYPE	ORDER #	BUY/SELL	SIZE	ENTRY PRICE	EXIT PRICE	CLOSE DATE /TIME	PROFIT/LOSS

NOTES:		NEW BALANCE

ORDER DATE/TIME	TYPE	ORDER #	BUY/SELL	SIZE	ENTRY PRICE	EXIT PRICE	CLOSE DATE /TIME	PROFIT/LOSS

NOTES:		NEW BALANCE

TRADING LOG

ORDER DATE/TIME	TYPE	ORDER #	BUY/ SELL	SIZE	ENTRY PRICE	EXIT PRICE	CLOSE DATE /TIME	PROFIT/ LOSS

NOTES:						NEW BALANCE	

ORDER DATE/TIME	TYPE	ORDER #	BUY/ SELL	SIZE	ENTRY PRICE	EXIT PRICE	CLOSE DATE /TIME	PROFIT/ LOSS

NOTES:						NEW BALANCE	

ORDER DATE/TIME	TYPE	ORDER #	BUY/ SELL	SIZE	ENTRY PRICE	EXIT PRICE	CLOSE DATE /TIME	PROFIT/ LOSS

NOTES.						NEW BALANCE	

ORDER DATE/TIME	TYPE	ORDER #	BUY/ SELL	SIZE	ENTRY PRICE	EXIT PRICE	CLOSE DATE /TIME	PROFIT/ LOSS

NOTES:						NEW BALANCE	

ORDER DATE/TIME	TYPE	ORDER #	BUY/ SELL	SIZE	ENTRY PRICE	EXIT PRICE	CLOSE DATE /TIME	PROFIT/ LOSS

NOTES:						NEW BALANCE	

TRADING LOG

ORDER DATE/TIME	TYPE	ORDER #	BUY/ SELL	SIZE	ENTRY PRICE	EXIT PRICE	CLOSE DATE /TIME	PROFIT/ LOSS

NOTES:				NEW BALANCE	

ORDER DATE/TIME	TYPE	ORDER #	BUY/ SELL	SIZE	ENTRY PRICE	EXIT PRICE	CLOSE DATE /TIME	PROFIT/ LOSS

NOTES:				NEW BALANCE	

ORDER DATE/TIME	TYPE	ORDER #	BUY/ SELL	SIZE	ENTRY PRICE	EXIT PRICE	CLOSE DATE /TIME	PROFIT/ LOSS

NOTES:				NEW BALANCE	

ORDER DATE/TIME	TYPE	ORDER #	BUY/ SELL	SIZE	ENTRY PRICE	EXIT PRICE	CLOSE DATE /TIME	PROFIT/ LOSS

NOTES:				NEW BALANCE	

ORDER DATE/TIME	TYPE	ORDER #	BUY/ SELL	SIZE	ENTRY PRICE	EXIT PRICE	CLOSE DATE /TIME	PROFIT/ LOSS

NOTES:				NEW BALANCE	

TRADING LOG

ORDER DATE/TIME	TYPE	ORDER #	BUY/ SELL	SIZE	ENTRY PRICE	EXIT PRICE	CLOSE DATE /TIME	PROFIT/ LOSS

NOTES:	NEW BALANCE

ORDER DATE/TIME	TYPE	ORDER #	BUY/ SELL	SIZE	ENTRY PRICE	EXIT PRICE	CLOSE DATE /TIME	PROFIT/ LOSS

NOTES:	NEW BALANCE

ORDER DATE/TIME	TYPE	ORDER #	BUY/ SELL	SIZE	ENTRY PRICE	EXIT PRICE	CLOSE DATE /TIME	PROFIT/ LOSS

NOTES:	NEW BALANCE

ORDER DATE/TIME	TYPE	ORDER #	BUY/ SELL	SIZE	ENTRY PRICE	EXIT PRICE	CLOSE DATE /TIME	PROFIT/ LOSS

NOTES:	NEW BALANCE

ORDER DATE/TIME	TYPE	ORDER #	BUY/ SELL	SIZE	ENTRY PRICE	EXIT PRICE	CLOSE DATE /TIME	PROFIT/ LOSS

NOTES:	NEW BALANCE

Made in the USA
Columbia, SC
16 December 2024